Chris Hart

DRAWING THE NEW ADVENTURE CARTOONS

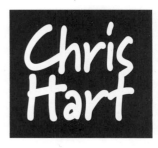

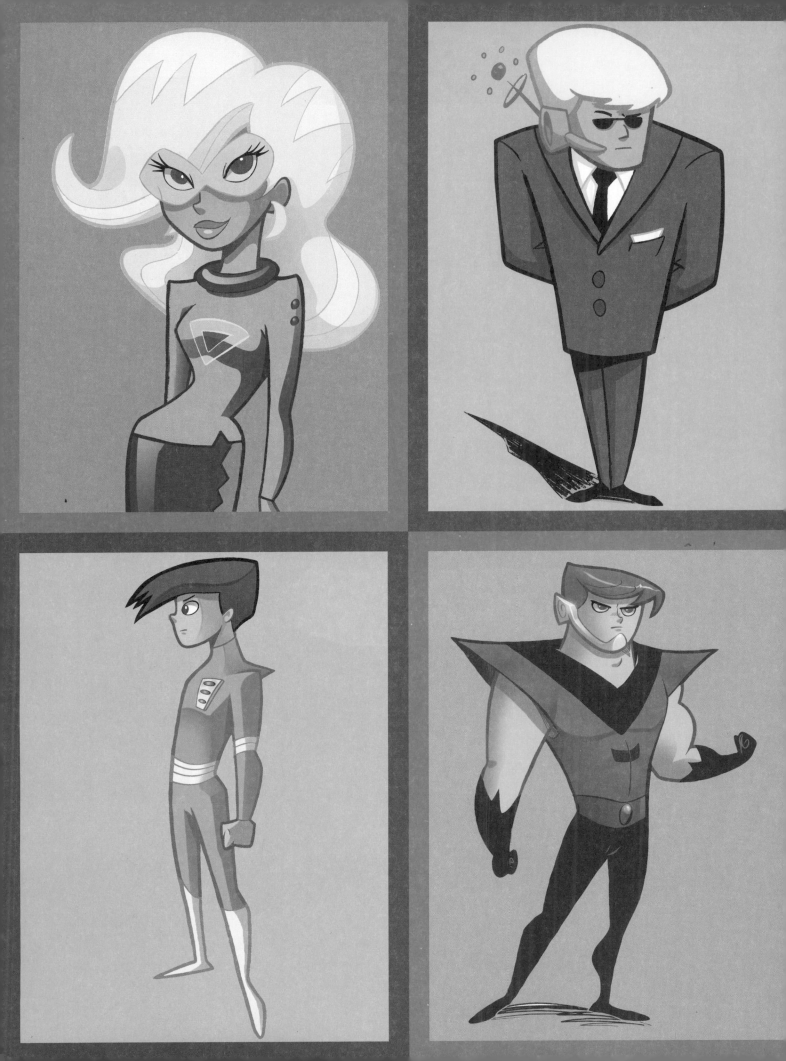

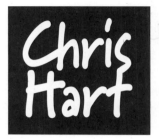

DRAWING THE NEW ADVENTURE CARTOONS

Cool Spies, Evil Guys and Action Heroes

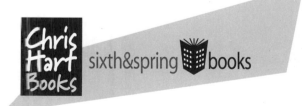

Chris Hart Books   sixth&spring books

233 Spring St.
New York, NY 10013

Editorial Director
ELAINE SILVERSTEIN

Book Design
DAVID WOLF

Book Division Manager
ERICA SMITH

Color
MADA DESIGN, INC.

Senior Editor
MICHELLE BREDESON

Additional Color
ROMULO FAJARDO

Art Director
DIANE LAMPHRON

Inks
FABIO LAGUNA

Associate Art Director
SHEENA T. PAUL

Copy Editor
KRISTINA SIGLER

President
ART JOINNIDES

Production Manager
DAVID JOINNIDES

Vice President, Publisher
TRISHA MALCOLM

Creative Director
JOE VIOR

Library of Congress Control Number: 2007907248

ISBN-13: 978-1-933027-60-9
ISBN-10: 1-933027-60-6

Manufactured in China

1 3 5 7 9 10 8 6 4 2

First Edition

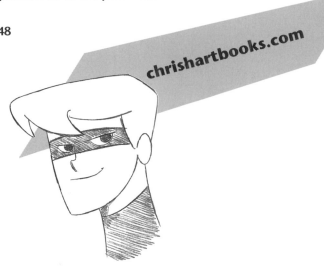

chrishartbooks.com

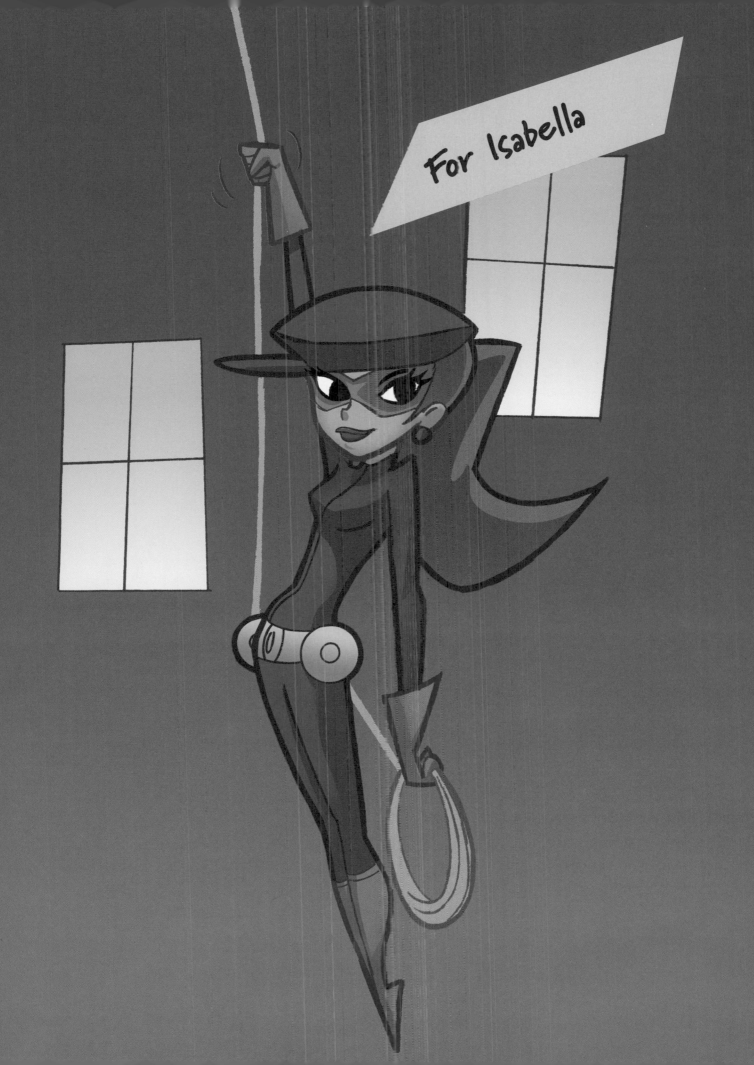

CONTENTS

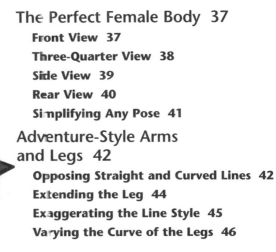

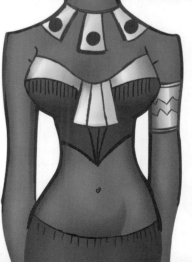

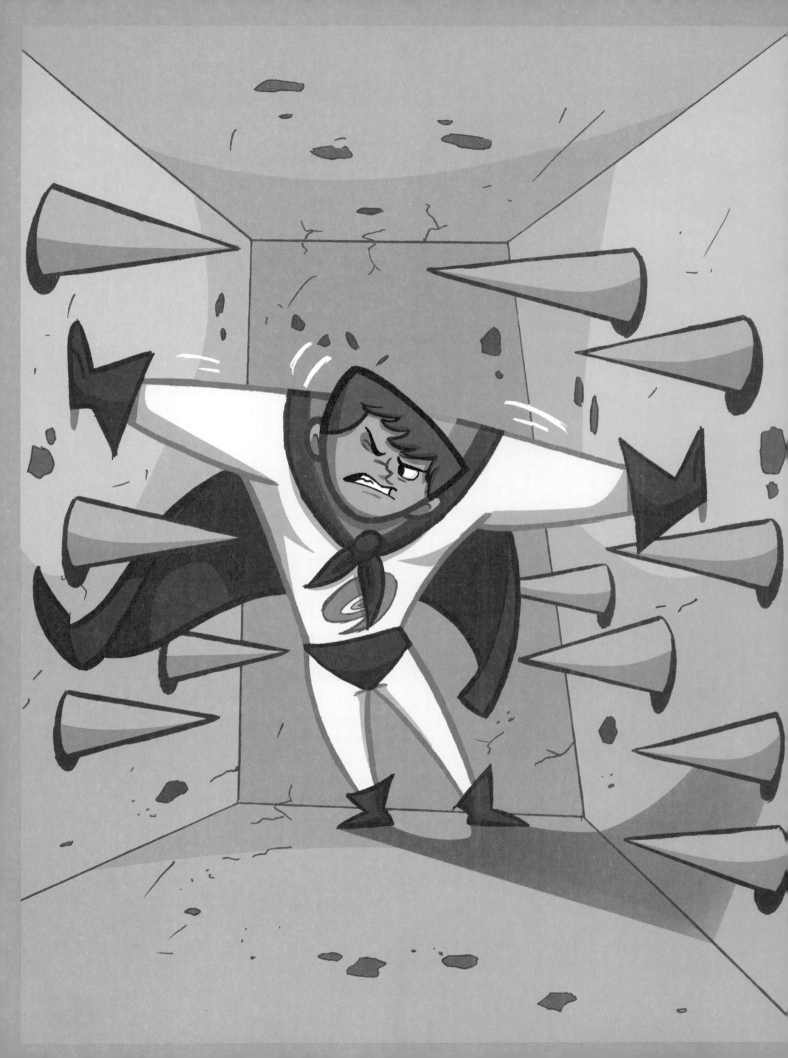

INTRODUCTION

Welcome to the exciting world of adventure-style cartooning! You've seen these eye-catching character types on popular animated TV shows, in blockbuster animated movies and in the pages of all the top comic books. Adventure-style cartooning is action-packed cartooning at its best, with lots of personality, humor and cutting-edge costume design thrown into the mix. All these elements combine to create a style that's in tremendous demand. You love to watch it, and you'll love to draw it.

The great thing about adventure-style cartooning is that the concepts are easy to grasp, especially since the instruction is supplemented by tons of visual hints. When I wrote this book, I tried to think of myself as a mentor—someone who stays right at your side, giving you professional insights all along the way, but with the clear and easy examples you expect from a Chris Hart book.

In this book, I'll take you through all the basics and then on to the coolest aspects of the style. These include body language and attitudes; opposing straight and curved body contours; expression charts; drawing the action along the action line; simplified body construction; and more

You'll learn how to create a host of charismatic characters: teen heroes, secret agents, beautiful spies, ruthless crime bosses, news reporters, diabolical scientists, costumed crime fighters and many more. And there's even a section on basic composition and layout to help you set up scenes and put your characters in action.

Hey, drawing has never been this much fun. And you're going to raise your skill level way up in the process, without even realizing it. Are you ready to get really good at this?

TEEN BOY HERO

While most kids are making money on their paper routes or Internet startups, our young hero keeps busy fighting crime. It's a thankless job. His grades may suffer. His girl may wonder where he is on Saturday night. His parents may even worry about his level of motivation. But someone's got to protect the city from all those villains.

Front View

Our young hero is earnest and purposeful, but with a soft, clean-cut look. No hard angles here! Luckily for us, this makes him easy to draw.

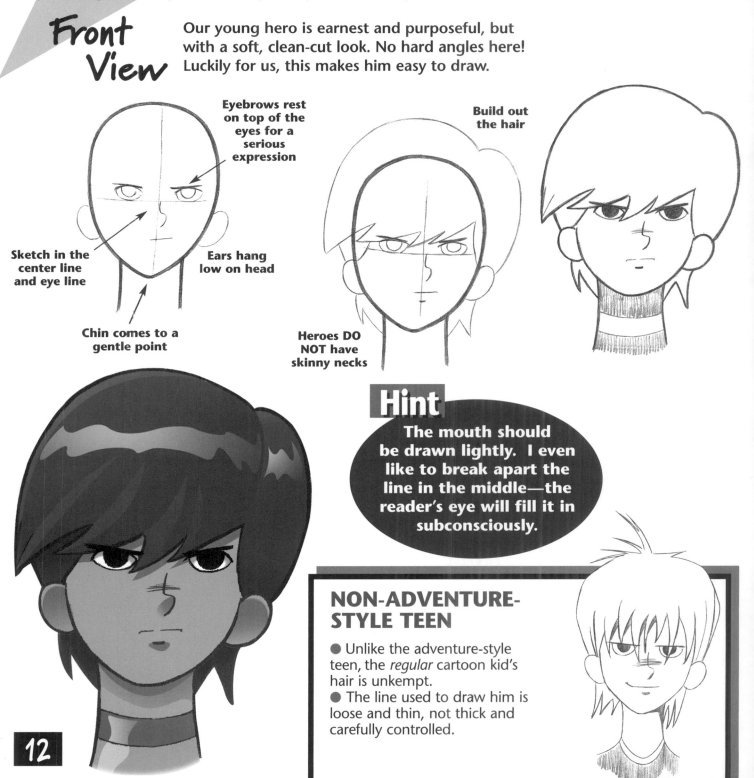

Eyebrows rest on top of the eyes for a serious expression

Sketch in the center line and eye line

Ears hang low on head

Chin comes to a gentle point

Build out the hair

Heroes DO NOT have skinny necks

Hint

The mouth should be drawn lightly. I even like to break apart the line in the middle—the reader's eye will fill it in subconsciously.

NON-ADVENTURE-STYLE TEEN

● Unlike the adventure-style teen, the *regular* cartoon kid's hair is unkempt.
● The line used to draw him is loose and thin, not thick and carefully controlled.

Three-Quarter View

Our hero's wide face makes this three-quarter view easy to draw—just follow the steps. It's important to begin by sketching in the center line. This helps you align the features on either side of the face.

Carve out the area between the forehead and the cheekbone

Notice that the bridge of the nose runs up and down the center line

Center line

Eye line

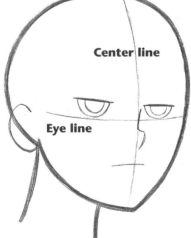

13

Side View

The side view, also called a "profile," gives the character a strong, chiseled look. The chin should be tucked down a bit (*a sign of determination*), and let that flap of hair hang loosely over his eyes. Even ordinary teenagers with no superpowers have the amazing ability to see through a headful of hair covering their eyes!

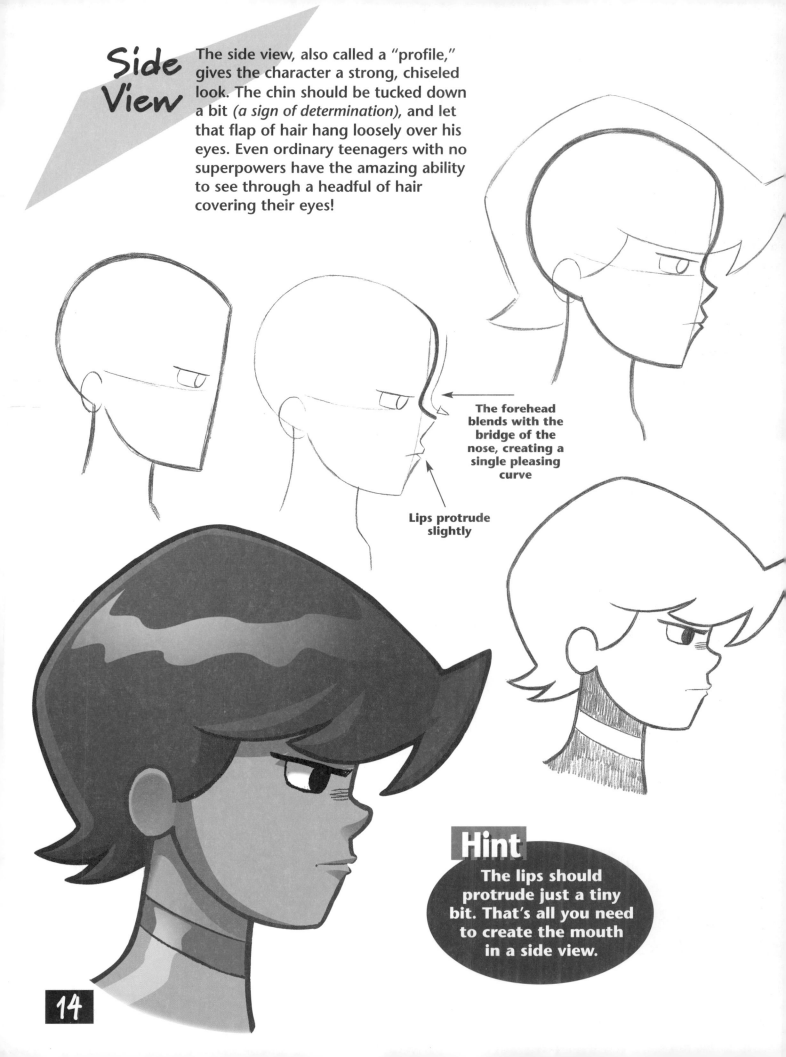

The forehead blends with the bridge of the nose, creating a single pleasing curve

Lips protrude slightly

Hint
The lips should protrude just a tiny bit. That's all you need to create the mouth in a side view.

Drawing the Head in Any Direction!

"How can I draw the same character in different positions, but keep it looking the same?" This is the second most common question I get asked as a professional cartoonist. (The first is "When are you going to pay me back?" but I'll answer that one later.)

Drawing a character at different angles is actually very easy. But in order to do it right, there's one "gotta." And here it is: You've gotta draw the basic construction first, before you add the features and the hair. The basic construction is the general outline of the head along with the center line and eye line, just as you've been practicing on the previous pages.

Front View Down

3/4 View Right Down

3/4 View Right Up

3/4 View Left Up

Front View Up

THE CHANGING SHAPE OF THE EYES

As the eye looks straight ahead, up or down, it actually changes shape. The pupil becomes rounder or more oval. The curve of the eyebrow also adjusts.

Straight Ahead   **Looking Up**   **Looking Down**

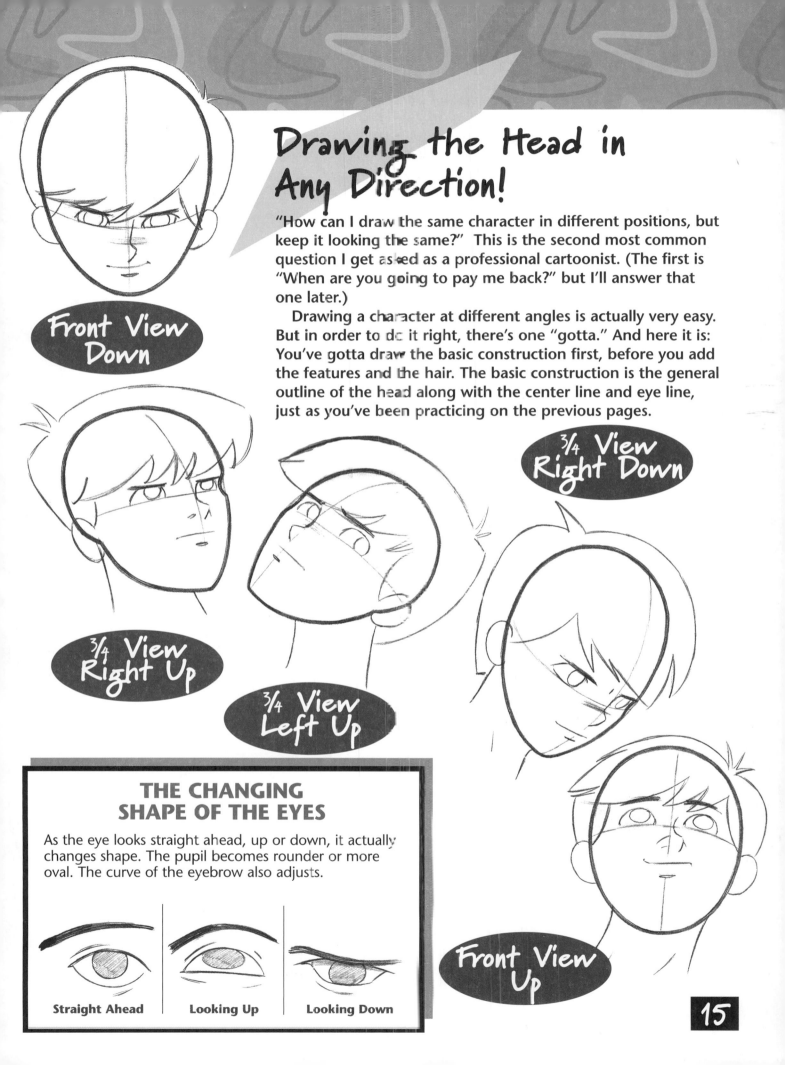

15

TEEN GIRL HERO

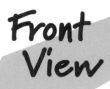
Front View

Our girl hero is on the side of good, so she should be pretty, but in a wholesome way. That means a roundish face. You don't have to shy away from long eyelashes or full lips—just don't make her overtly sultry. Over-the-top allure is for female villains, who use their appeal to lure good guys to their demise.

When drawing this character, your line quality should be thick but spare to create a simplified, clean look. Even her hair, with the ruffled bangs, is perfectly symmetrical.

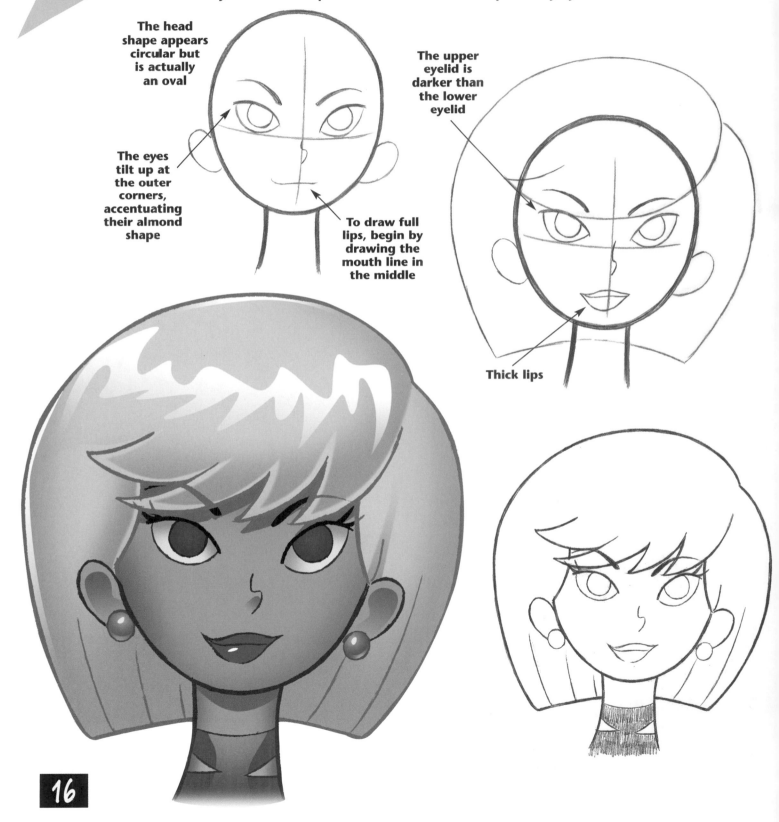

The head shape appears circular but is actually an oval

The eyes tilt up at the outer corners, accentuating their almond shape

To draw full lips, begin by drawing the mouth line in the middle

The upper eyelid is darker than the lower eyelid

Thick lips

Three-Quarter View

With this youthful character, the face stays wide in the three-quarter view. This makes her easier to draw than bony characters or characters with angular faces.

Hint

In the three-quarter view, the far eye is always positioned *much closer* to the bridge of the nose than the near eye.

Hair sweeps back around face, at an angle

An overbite is an attractive look for characters with full lips

THE CHEEK BUMP-OUT

Cartoonists use the cheek bump-out to fill out the character's face and give her a youthful look.

Is it ever omitted? Sure, if you want the character to look more retro. As you progress through this book, you'll see that some characters look funnier with the bump-out, while others look cooler without it. As an artist, the choice is yours. But this is another important tool for you to have in your arsenal.

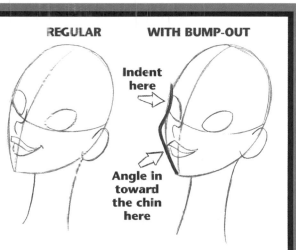

REGULAR   WITH BUMP-OUT

Indent here

Angle in toward the chin here

It's easy to make the side view look flat and angular. So be on your guard to fight against that. How? Simple: work those gentle curves into the forehead, nose and chin—and especially the underside of the jaw.

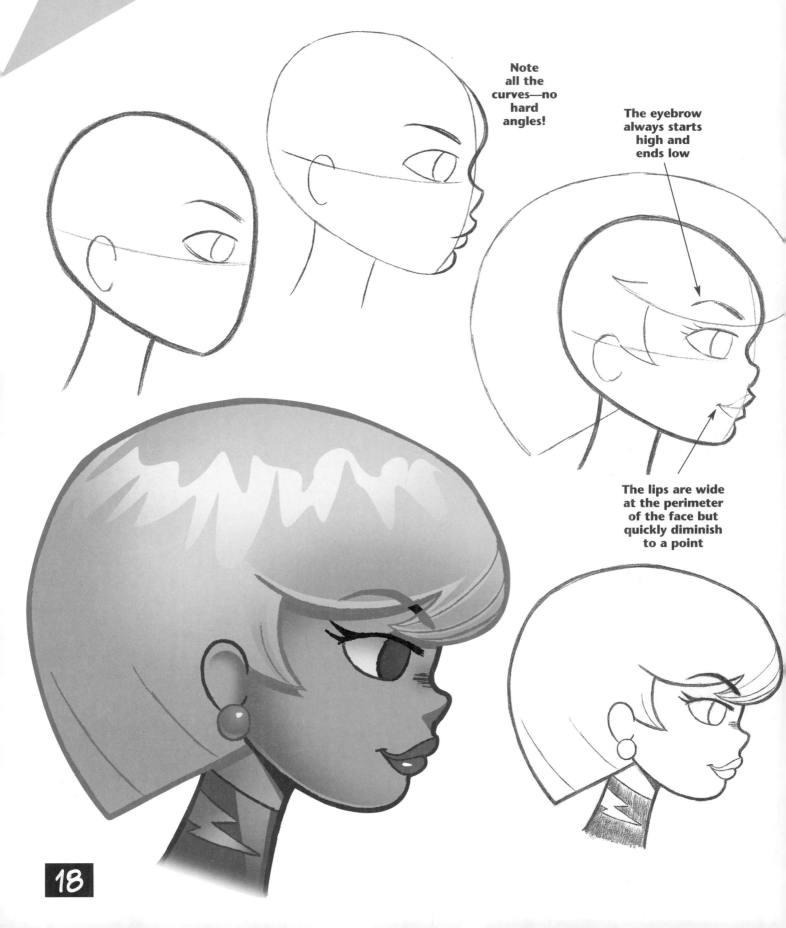

Note all the curves—no hard angles!

The eyebrow always starts high and ends low

The lips are wide at the perimeter of the face but quickly diminish to a point

¾ View Left Up

¾ Rear View

Turning the Head

Now that we've been digging through some solid cartooning information, take a general glance at this page with your newly educated eye. Notice how the same character's head is tilted at various angles but the character remains recognizably the same. I've accomplished this by using the center line and eye line to place the character's features in each sketch.

Be sure to sketch the construction first, then fill in the unique characteristics second. That's the secret!

¾ View Right Down

¾ View Right Up

¾ View Left Down

19

AGING YOUR CHARACTER

Adventure-style heroes are very often kids, teens or young adults. And each age has specific physical traits. Using these traits in your drawings will let your audience identify your hero's age clearly and immediately.

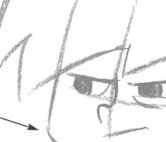

Kid

Head is as wide as it is tall

Giant hair

Cheek positioned low on face

Tiny or no chin

Skinny neck

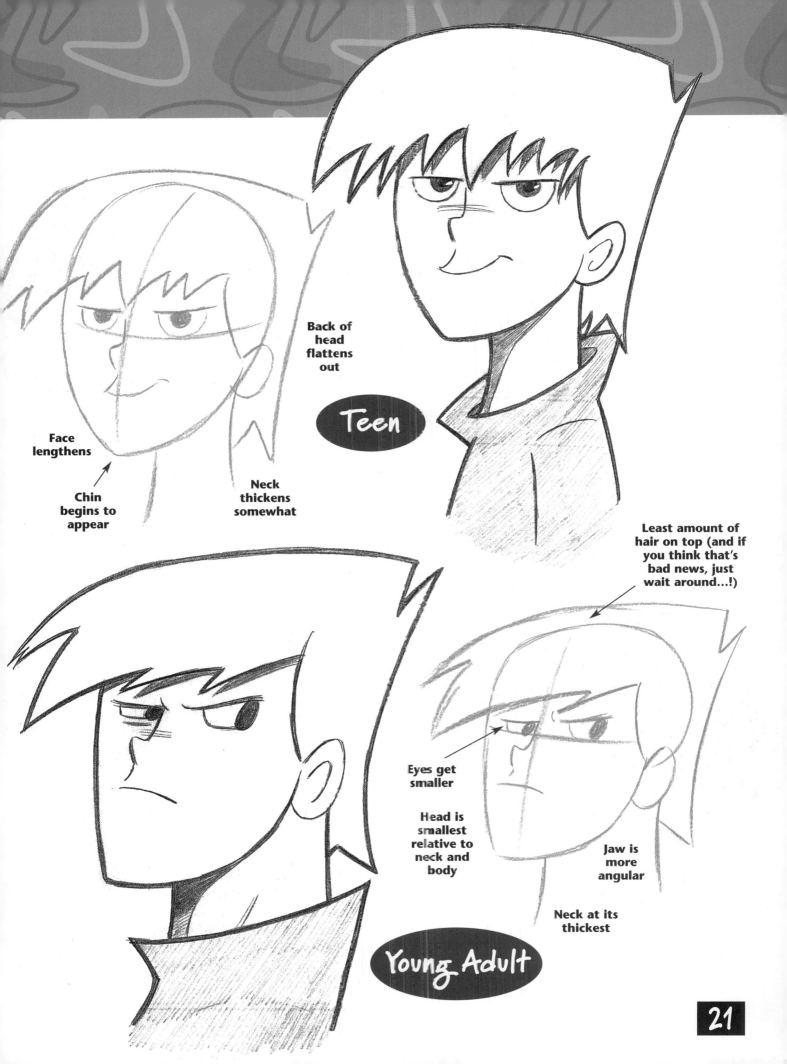

Face
lengthens

Chin
begins to
appear

Back of
head
flattens
out

Teen

Neck
thickens
somewhat

Least amount of
hair on top (and if
you think that's
bad news, just
wait around...!)

Eyes get
smaller

Head is
smallest
relative to
neck and
body

Jaw is
more
angular

Neck at its
thickest

Young Adult

COOL TEEN BOY

Older teens—ages 17 to 19—are a popular subset of adventure-style characters. Characters of this age are the ones that younger kids idolize—the "cool" teens. Older teens, while still youthful, are also robust and powerful. They are at the top of their form.

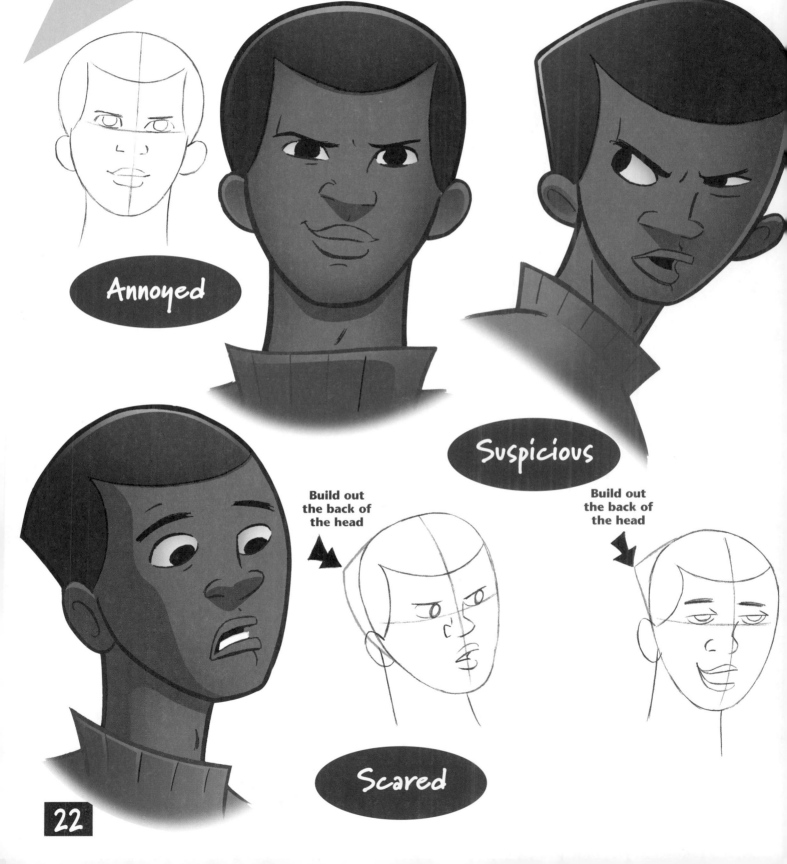

Annoyed

Suspicious

Build out the back of the head

Scared

Build out the back of the head

OLDER TEEN GIRL

This bright-eyed teen is 16 to 18 years old, well past the tween years but not yet an adult. She retains youthful features—a ponytail, an extra-round face and a large forehead—but her eyes are not as huge as those of a younger girl.

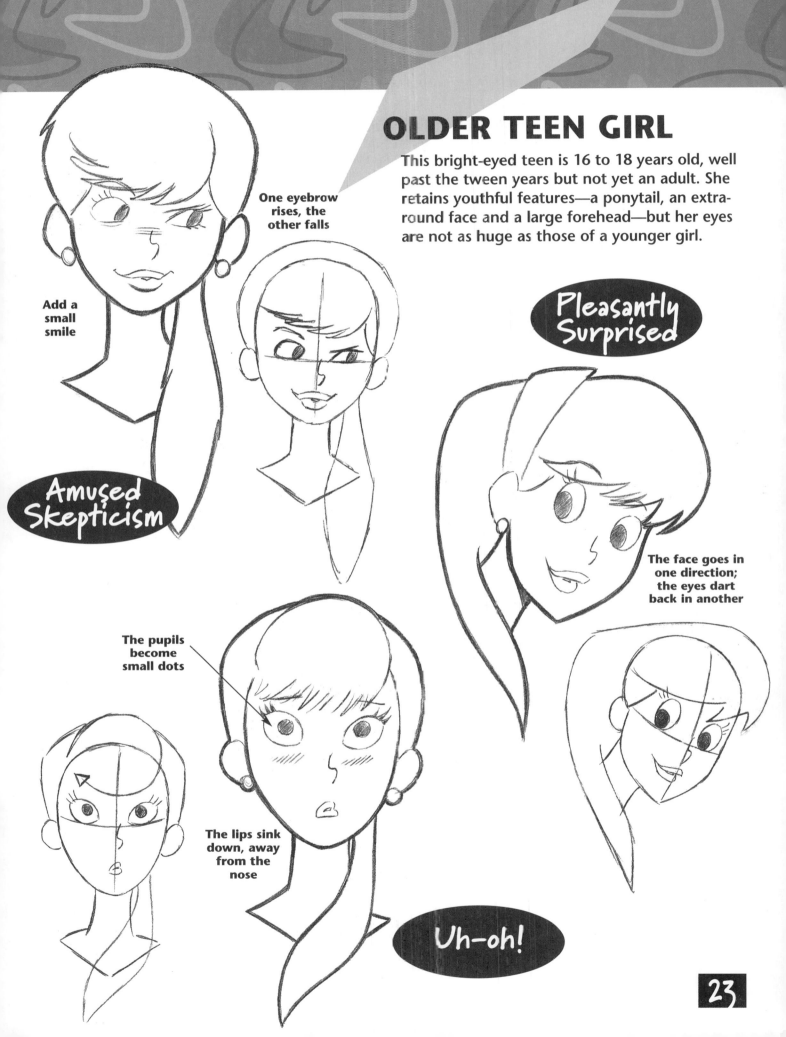

One eyebrow rises, the other falls

Add a small smile

Amused Skepticism

Pleasantly Surprised

The face goes in one direction; the eyes dart back in another

The pupils become small dots

The lips sink down, away from the nose

Uh-oh!

23

YOUNG LEADING MAN

An action hero who switches identity from a regular Joe into a super crime fighter has to have a masculine look. Then again, your star might be a charismatic leading man who doesn't need superpowers. Either way, a little heroic star power goes a long way in providing that *extra something* that turns a character into an audience favorite.

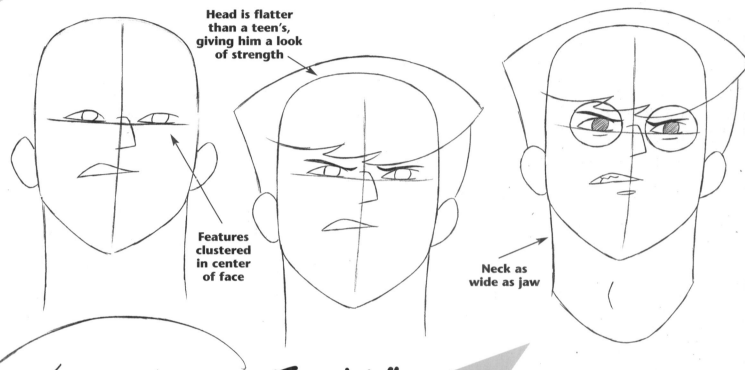

Head is flatter than a teen's, giving him a look of strength

Features clustered in center of face

Neck as wide as jaw

Front View

Compared with the young teen, the adult has a *larger chin* and a *smaller forehead*. But the thing that will help your drawing the most is to draw the nose *to one side or the other*, either left or right, rather than straight on.

Drawing the nose straight on makes it look flat and unappealing. So we move it to the side. Is that cheating? Yes. But don't worry—cartoonists cheat like this all the time!

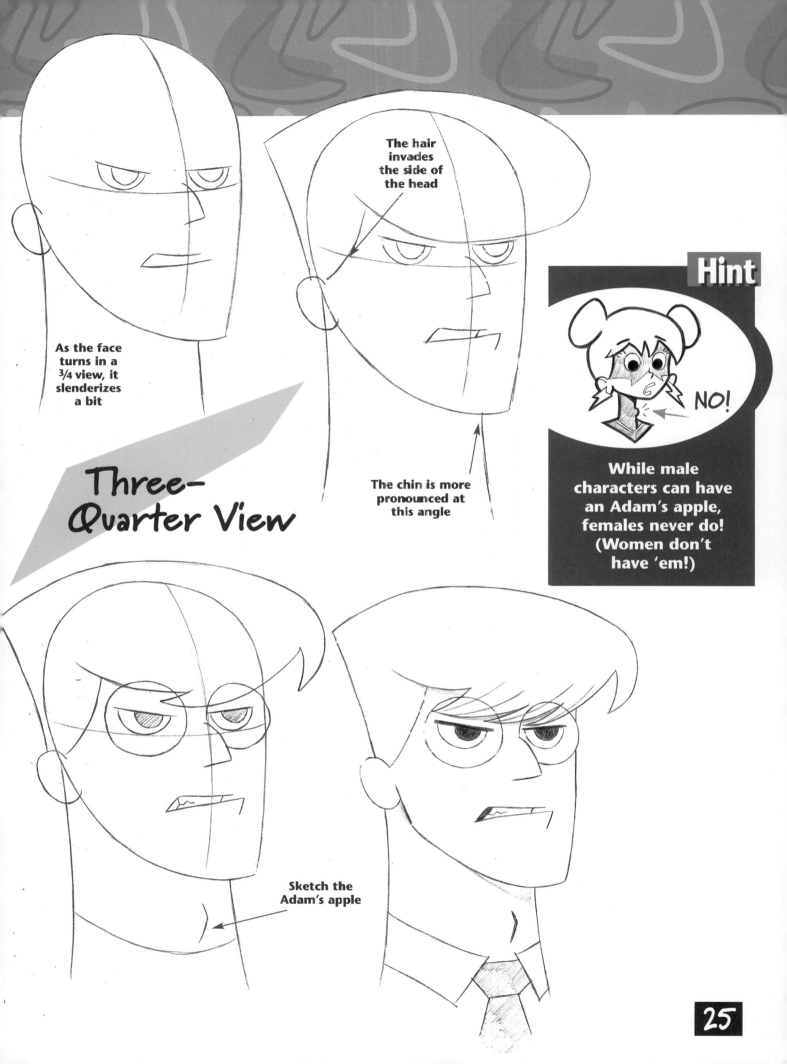

The hair invades the side of the head

As the face turns in a ¾ view, it slenderizes a bit

Three-Quarter View

The chin is more pronounced at this angle

Hint

NO!

While male characters can have an Adam's apple, females never do! (Women don't have 'em!)

Sketch the Adam's apple

25

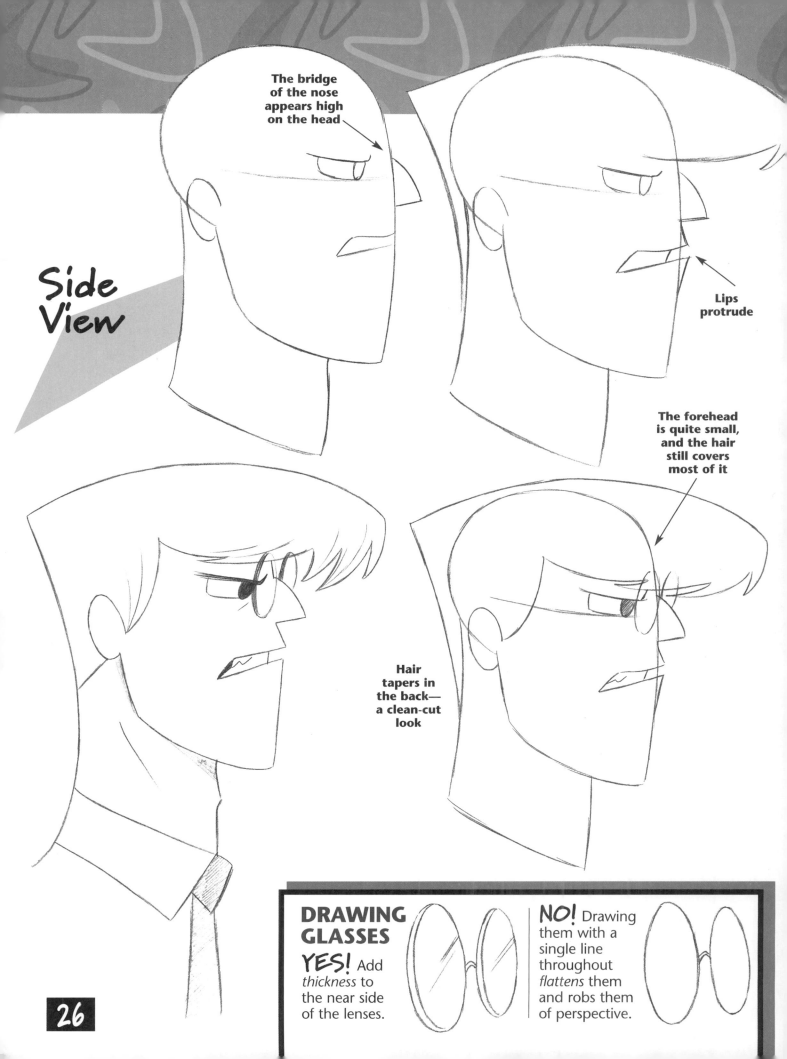

The bridge of the nose appears high on the head

Side View

Lips protrude

The forehead is quite small, and the hair still covers most of it

Hair tapers in the back— a clean-cut look

DRAWING GLASSES

YES! Add *thickness* to the near side of the lenses.

NO! Drawing them with a single line throughout *flattens* them and robs them of perspective.

26

YOUNG FEMALE LEAD
Front View

Build the hair out even farther than the already wide cranium

Wider here

Narrower here

The line of the eyebrow is a continuation of the bridge of the nose

The eyelashes are clumped rather than drawn as individual lashes

Hint

Note the full, attractive lips. To draw the smile, first draw the mouth line straight across, only curving up at the very ends. Second, fill out the lips.

Hint

The top eyelashes should be drawn brushing UP and away from the eye; the bottom eyelashes should be drawn brushing DOWN and away from the eye. On a glamorous character, *bunch the eyelashes together* instead of drawing each individual eyelash as a single line.

Three-Quarter View

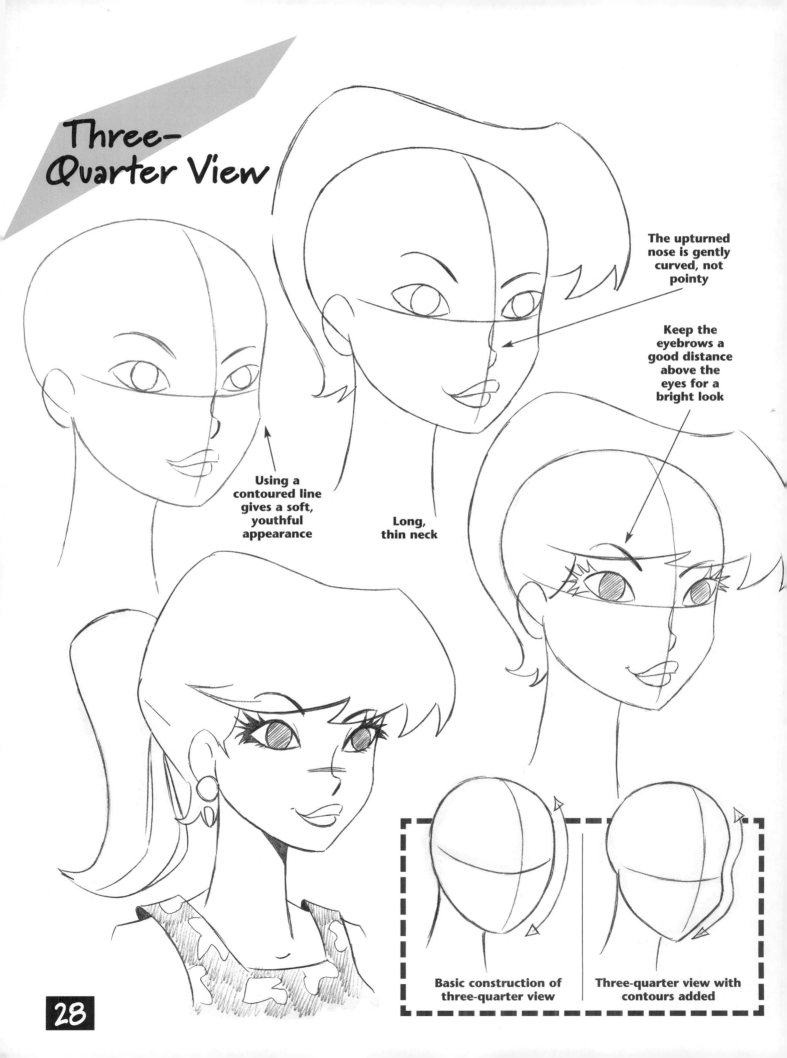

The upturned nose is gently curved, not pointy

Keep the eyebrows a good distance above the eyes for a bright look

Using a contoured line gives a soft, youthful appearance

Long, thin neck

Basic construction of three-quarter view

Three-quarter view with contours added

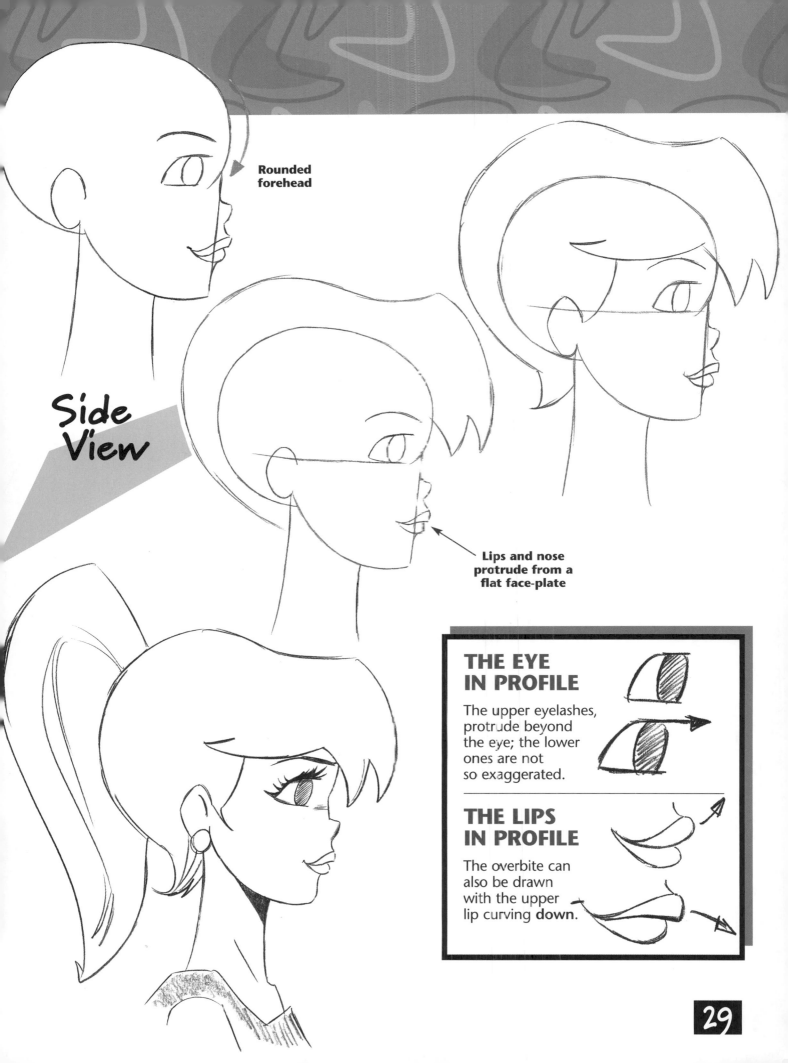

Rounded forehead

Side View

Lips and nose protrude from a flat face-plate

THE EYE IN PROFILE

The upper eyelashes, protrude beyond the eye; the lower ones are not so exaggerated.

THE LIPS IN PROFILE

The overbite can also be drawn with the upper lip curving **down**.

SPY MASKS

Spy masks add the cool factor to spy outfits. Masks are usually unisex—interchangeable for guys and gals. They can be plain or fancy. With a mask on, no one can identify you. (Actually, any *reader* can easily identify you—it's the *other characters* in the story who suddenly become numbskulled and can't put it together. But that's what makes the stories work—and audiences and readers alike go along for the ride!)

We'll examine some of the more popular styles as well as a few more esoteric ones. You can combine types to make your own unique mask or design one from scratch.

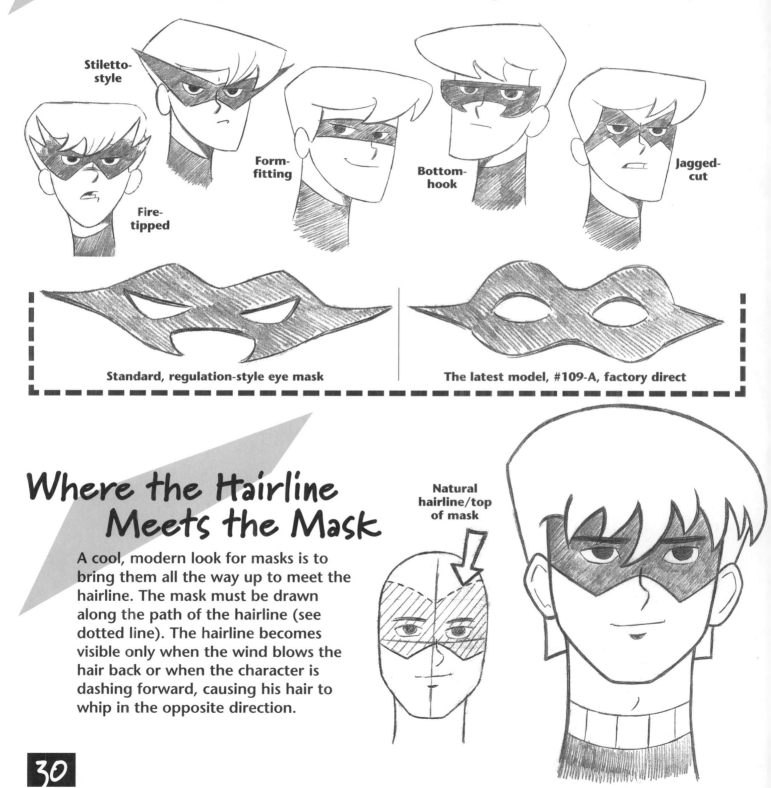

Stiletto-style

Fire-tipped

Form-fitting

Bottom-hook

Jagged-cut

Standard, regulation-style eye mask

The latest model, #109-A, factory direct

Where the Hairline Meets the Mask

A cool, modern look for masks is to bring them all the way up to meet the hairline. The mask must be drawn along the path of the hairline (see dotted line). The hairline becomes visible only when the wind blows the hair back or when the character is dashing forward, causing his hair to whip in the opposite direction.

Natural hairline/top of mask

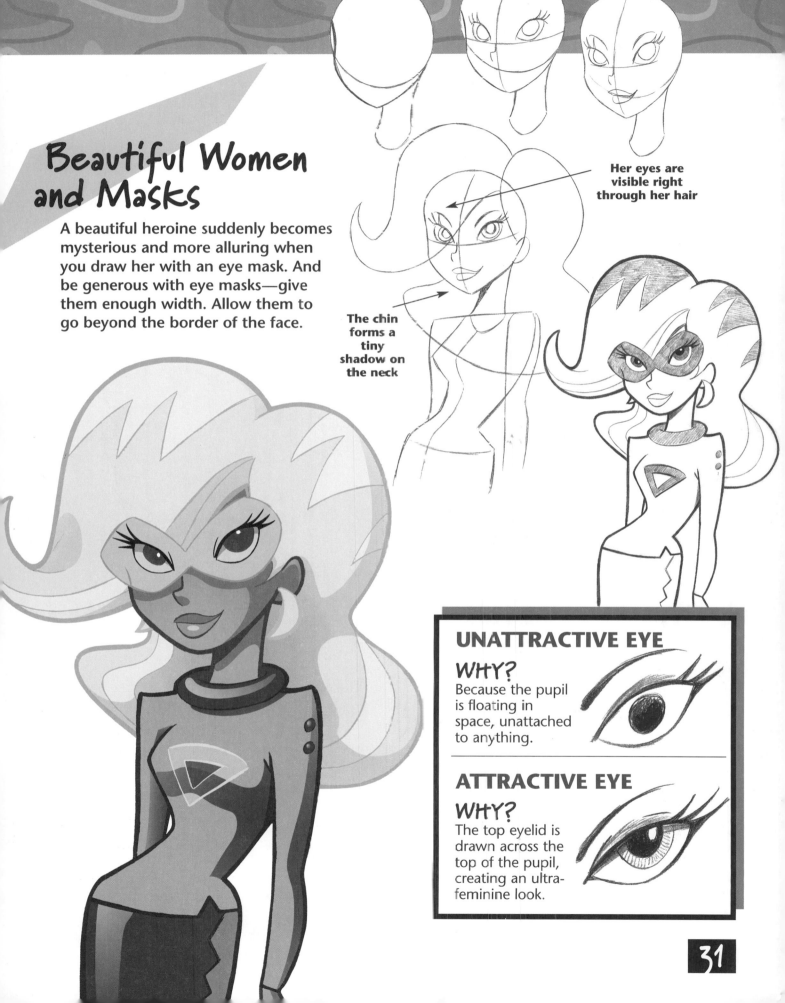

Beautiful Women and Masks

A beautiful heroine suddenly becomes mysterious and more alluring when you draw her with an eye mask. And be generous with eye masks—give them enough width. Allow them to go beyond the border of the face.

Her eyes are visible right through her hair

The chin forms a tiny shadow on the neck

UNATTRACTIVE EYE

WHY?
Because the pupil is floating in space, unattached to anything.

ATTRACTIVE EYE

WHY?
The top eyelid is drawn across the top of the pupil, creating an ultra-feminine look.

DRAWING THE TEEN ACTION BODY

He looks like a combo of gymnast and rock star, wrapped up in a uniform made of plutonium and tinfoil. Is he hard to draw? Well, no, because to create this appealing look, you use a basic retro approach, which happens to be easy to do. In fact, if you try to complicate things, the character will lose its visual appeal. Keep it simple!

Front View

Side View

THE NECK AND CHEST

Let's begin by focusing on the upper torso, which is important because it's the basis for the structure of the entire body. You can define four key areas of the neck and chest with only a few lines:

- Neck
- Chest
- Collarbone
- Shoulders

THE MALE HERO'S BODY

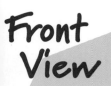
Keep the initial construction simple—you don't get points for complicating it. Remember, you use this initial sketch for your own reference. If you make it too complex, you're more likely to try to skip this step.

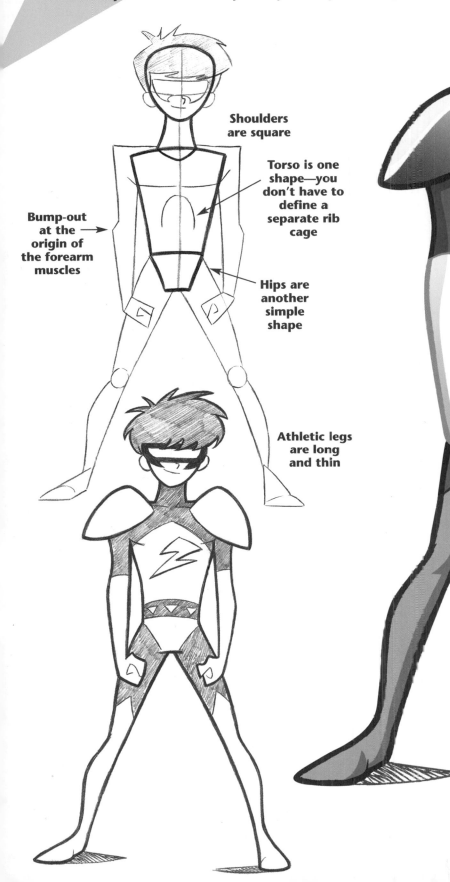

Shoulders are square

Torso is one shape—you don't have to define a separate rib cage

Bump-out at the origin of the forearm muscles

Hips are another simple shape

Athletic legs are long and thin

Three-Quarter View

Most how-to-draw books don't include the three-quarter full-body view. Usually, it's front and side only and occasionally a rear view. But how often does someone stand directly facing you, in a front view? Usually, people stand off to one side or the other, so it's important to learn to draw this most natural angle as well.

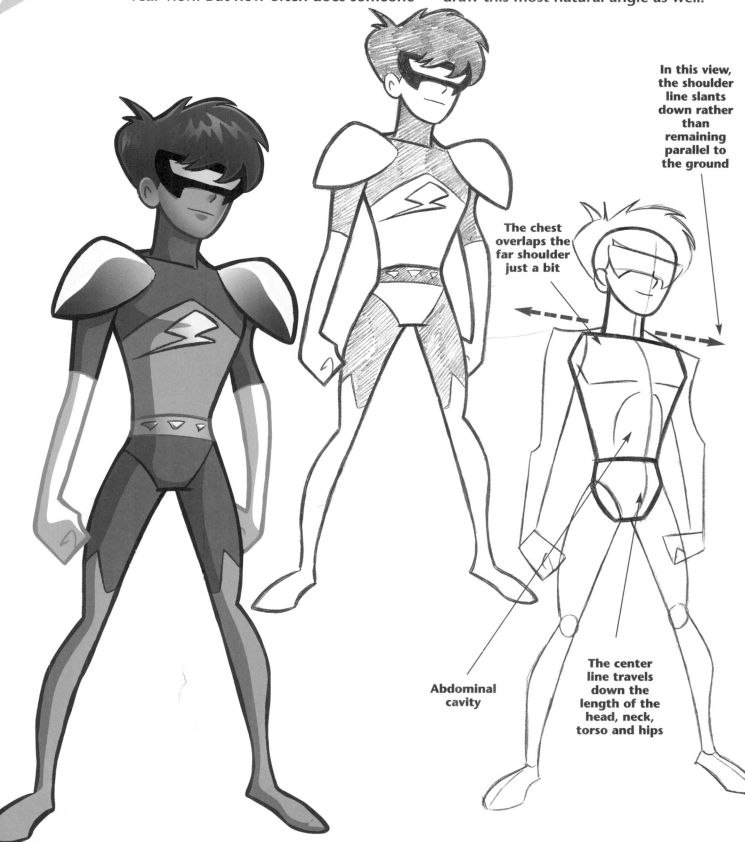

In this view, the shoulder line slants down rather than remaining parallel to the ground

The chest overlaps the far shoulder just a bit

Abdominal cavity

The center line travels down the length of the head, neck, torso and hips

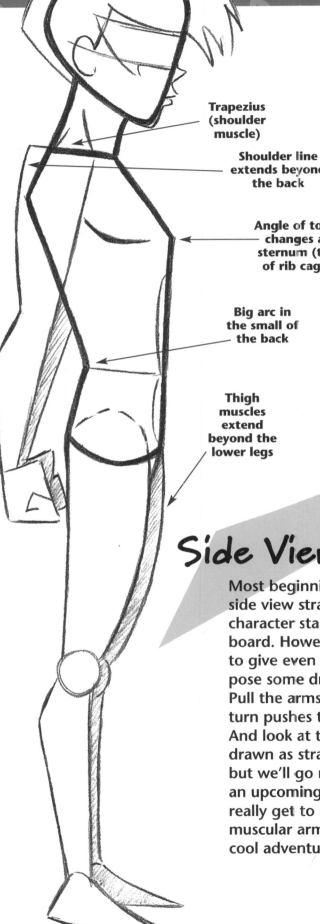

Trapezius
(shoulder
muscle)

Shoulder line
extends beyond
the back

Angle of torso
changes at
sternum (top
of rib cage)

Big arc in
the small of
the back

Thigh
muscles
extend
beyond the
lower legs

Side View

Most beginning artists draw the side view straight up, with the character standing stiff as a board. However, you can learn to give even a simple standing pose some dramatic tension. Pull the arms back, which in turn pushes the chest forward. And look at the legs: they aren't drawn as straight lines, either—but we'll go more into that in an upcoming chapter, so you'll really get to master drawing the muscular arms and legs in the cool adventure style.

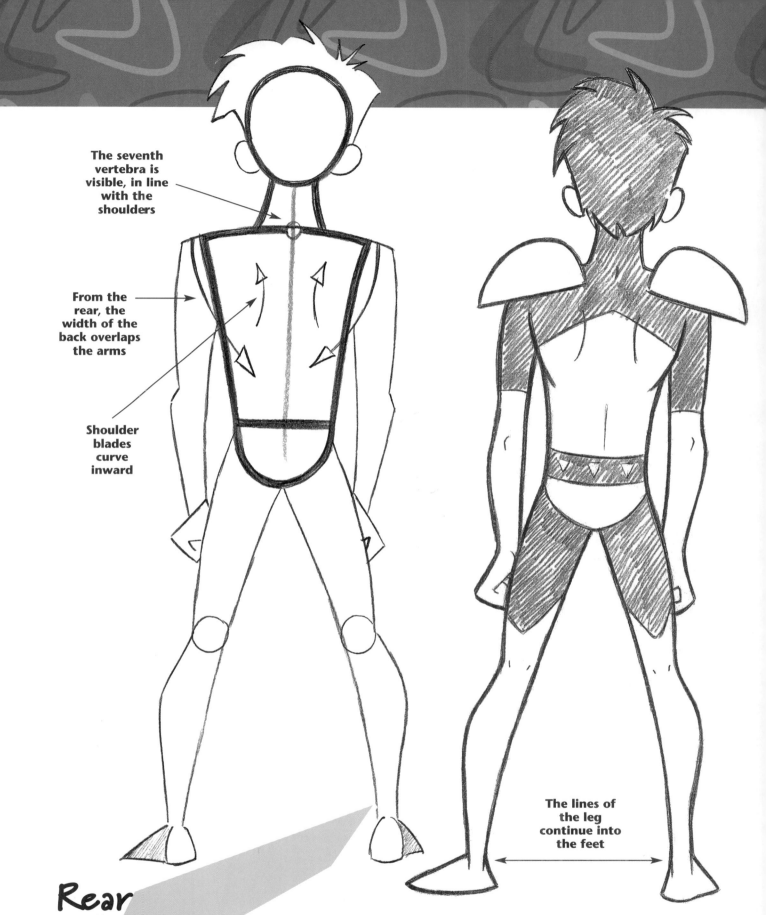

The seventh vertebra is visible, in line with the shoulders

From the rear, the width of the back overlaps the arms

Shoulder blades curve inward

The lines of the leg continue into the feet

Rear View

Here's a subtle but important point about drawing the feet in the rear view. Don't draw one foot pointing directly left and the other pointing directly right, because that would make the character look like he's about to tip over! Instead, make the feet point ahead at 45-degree angles.

THE PERFECT FEMALE BODY

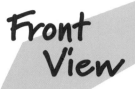

Exaggeration is key to drawing the female hero, and repeated shapes are how you get there. Think ovals! Draw the head, rib cage and hips as ovals that vary in size and shape. Draw the hips a generous size. This won't make your character appear chubby if you complement the hips with a tiny waistline. The legs, too, are fully shaped—never skinny. However, be sure to offset this by extending their length. All of these techniques result in a cartoony look as well as an attractive and heroically built character.

Oval or circle for head

Oval for rib cage

Oval for hips

Hint

Drawing the feet in front was hard for me until I learned this trick: Slope the outside of the feet, and group the toes into a mound that overlaps the rest of the foot.

Three-Quarter View

To draw the three-quarter view, first draw the basic construction and then sketch in the center line. Trust me, it will make your life easier. The center line anchors the features and anatomy in place.

Squared shoulders are a good look, and a stylistic choice I recommend

The near breast is drawn inside the torso, the far one in profile

The tummy indents in the middle

Side View

Yep, the rib cage and the hips are two separate shapes connected by the midsection. However, the torso can also be seen as one solid shape. Eventually—not now, and not right away, but eventually—you'll feel comfortable drawing the entire torso without first sketching the rib cage and hips.

However, when a pose is complex, you can return to the basics to solve it. Just think—you are learning, right now, how to construct the entire body. Once you familiarize yourself with this way of drawing, there won't be a pose you can't build. The body will fit together like a jigsaw puzzle.

Visualize the entire torso as a single shape

Female legs bend slightly backward

PENCIL SKETCH

Here's the way I sketch out a first rough drawing. Notice that I still use underlying constructions, as shown in the head shape, elbows and shoulder joints. The lines are bold and dark. Don't use short, choppy or feathery lines to sketch. Stay loose!

39

Rear View

Narrow is the key word for this view. Give your female hero a narrow back and narrow her legs through her knees. Also, even though you can't see the front of her head, I like to show her bangs and ponytail. The only way to make this happen is to draw them off to one side.

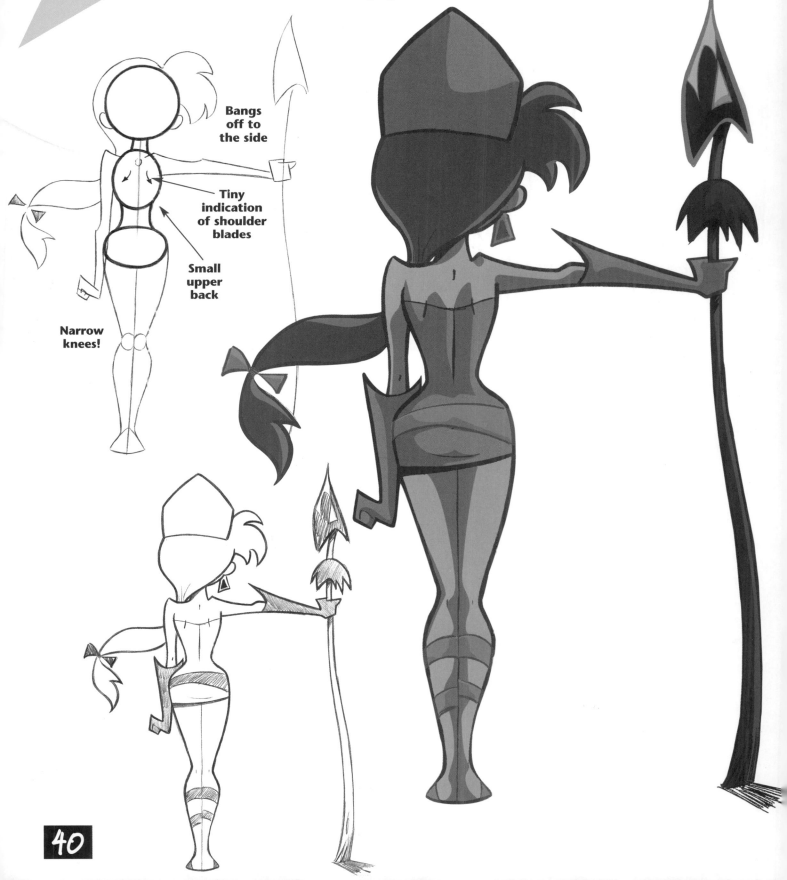

Bangs off to the side

Tiny indication of shoulder blades

Small upper back

Narrow knees!

Simplifying Any Pose

How can you learn to translate the standing poses we've studied in this chapter so far into **action** poses? I mean, that's the *real* question, isn't it?

To show you how, I've taken a basic female figure and posed her expressively using front, side and three-quarter views. Notice how each pose is based on our basic construction method. This method not only helps make your characters fit together smoothly—it also makes them simpler to draw in action poses!

ADVENTURE-STYLE ARMS AND LEGS

One signature technique for adventure-style cartooning has to do with drawing the arms and legs.

It is super-easy, and once you learn it, it makes a **HUGE** difference in your drawings.

Opposing Straight and Curved Lines

Nothing on the body is exactly ruler-straight. When you draw a limb, such as a forearm, you normally draw two lines: the inner and outer lines. Both lines are slightly curved.

Get ready for a change. In the adventure style, you draw one of those curved lines straight and the other very curved. You end up with opposing straight and curved lines.

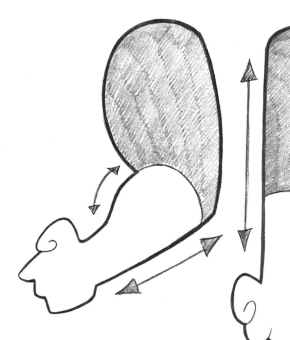

ARM BENT
When the arm is bent, the inner line is curved and the outer line is straight.

ARM STRAIGHT
When the arm is held straight, the inner line is straight and the outer line is curved.

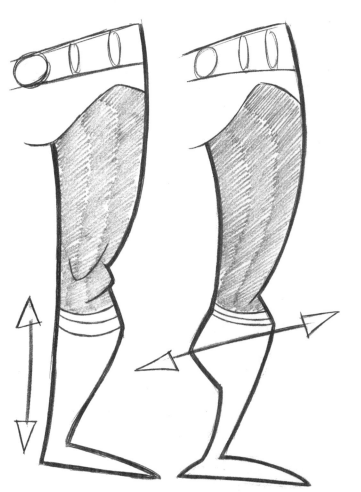

CLASSIC ADVENTURE-STYLE LEG
When the leg is locked, the inner line is straight and the outer line is curved. Note that the interior calf muscle is cut off.

VARIATION
If you want to show the entire calf muscle on the interior side, draw it higher on the outside and lower on the inside.

BICEPS NEED NOT APPLY

In this variation, the bent arm has a second curve to indicate a bicep. But this is not necessary. A single curve, as shown above, is sufficient.

Now let's look at the huge difference this technique makes. Compare the regular way of drawing arms and legs with the adventure-style way.

ADVENTURE STYLE
Notice the opposing straight lines and curves

REGULAR WAY (CURVES UPON CURVES)
It works, but it's not as sharp, not as cutting-edge as opposing straight and curved lines, is it?

Extending the Leg

In the adventure style, a single straight line extends down the leg and to the tip of the foot.

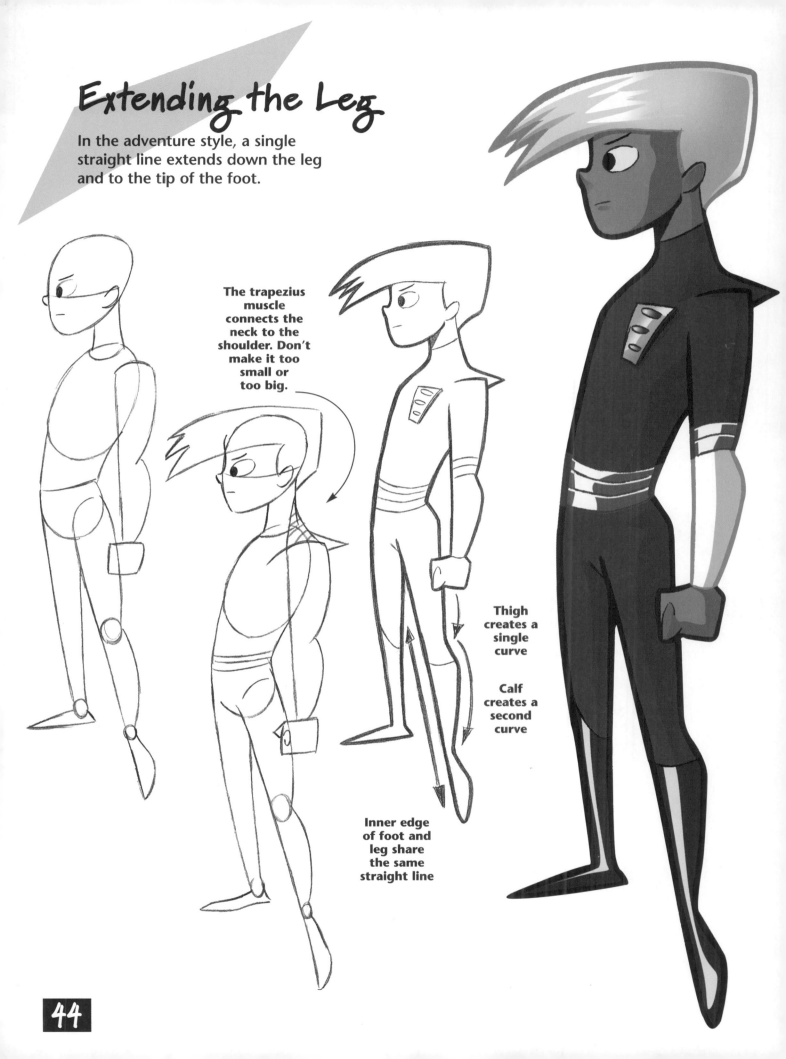

The trapezius muscle connects the neck to the shoulder. Don't make it too small or too big.

Thigh creates a single curve

Calf creates a second curve

Inner edge of foot and leg share the same straight line

Exaggerating the Line Style

The bigger the character's muscles, the more you can exaggerate the opposing straight and curved lines. The straight lines provide the contrast that prevents the figure from becoming a boring series of repeated bumps.

In this character, each straight line has its corresponding curve, making the whole figure look dynamic.

A Straight **B** Curved

Varying the Curve of the Legs

Just when you learn a new rule, I offer a new variation. But how good a teacher would I be if I left out a cool technique just to be consistent?

Here we go: Sometimes you want to exaggerate the length of a character's legs. And a good technique for doing that is to add even more curve to the *lower* legs. That may mean eliminating the straight lines *completely* from that part, and that part alone, of the leg.

Notice in the example below how this character's lower right leg has lost all its straight lines—it's entirely made up of curved lines—while the left leg retains the opposing straight and curved lines.

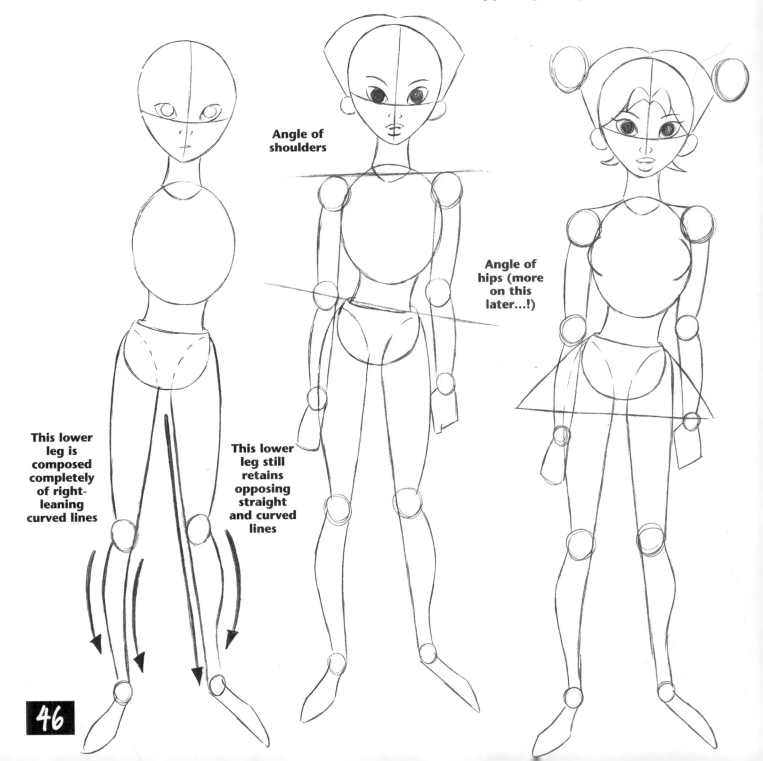

Angle of shoulders

Angle of hips (more on this later...!)

This lower leg is composed completely of right-leaning curved lines

This lower leg still retains opposing straight and curved lines

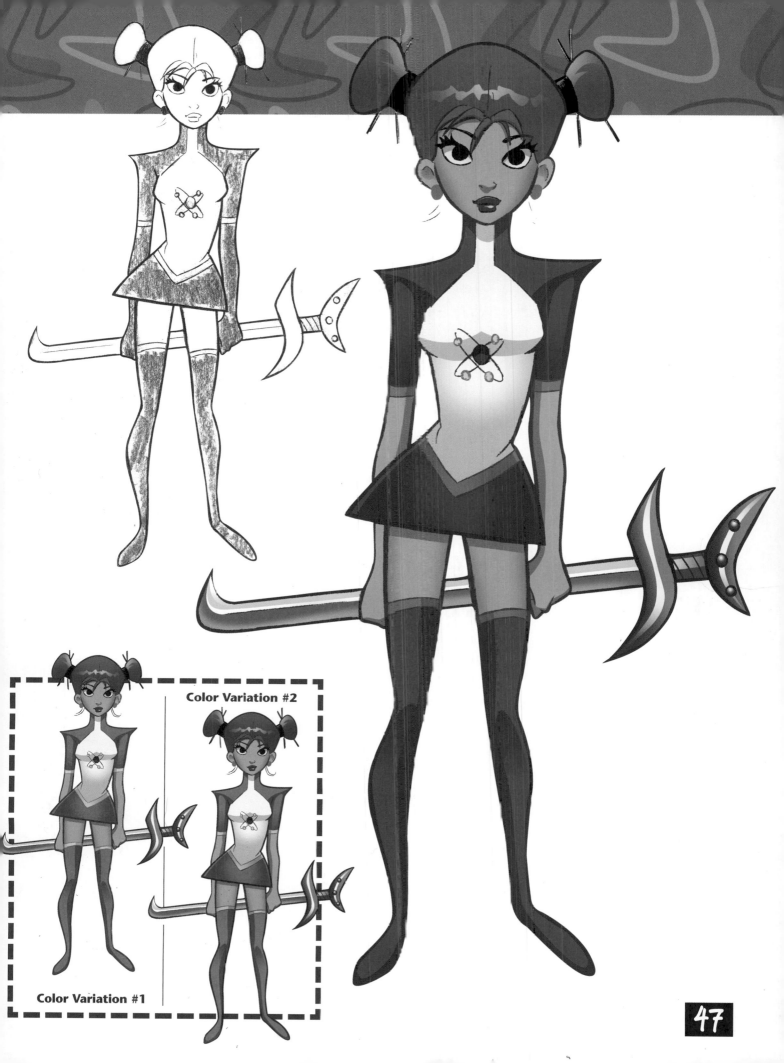

Color Variation #2

Color Variation #1

USING BODY LANGUAGE TO CONVEY EMOTION

An emotional connection needs to occur when you draw. Feelings are intrinsic to creativity. Pause before you draw, and think of how you feel when you perform an action.

For example, what if you were frightened? Perhaps you would lift your hands to your face in fear. Your body would have a surge of feeling running through it.

While focusing on that feeling, draw a character who feels that emotion. As you draw, use that feeling as your guide. When you look at your rough sketch, does it reflect the feeling of fear in your gut as you imagined it? If it does, then you have drawn it effectively. If it doesn't, try again, this time being more careful to include gestures and actions specific to that feeling.

This is the key to drawing body language: use the feeling in your gut as your guide!

POSITIVE AND NEGATIVE EMOTIONAL STATES

In cartooning, a positive emotional state is a forceful one— not necessarily a cheerful one. And as you've probably guessed, a negative emotional state is a passive one. Therefore, **positive emotional states** are represented with *forward-leaning postures*. **Negative emotional states** call for *backward-leaning postures*. Sometimes, all that means is a slight inward curving of the chest. Finally, **neutral emotional states** call for *erect postures*.

Neutral Pose— Affable

This character's emotional state is neutral, so he's standing more or less straight up and down. The hands tucked deeply into his pockets depict a casual demeanor.

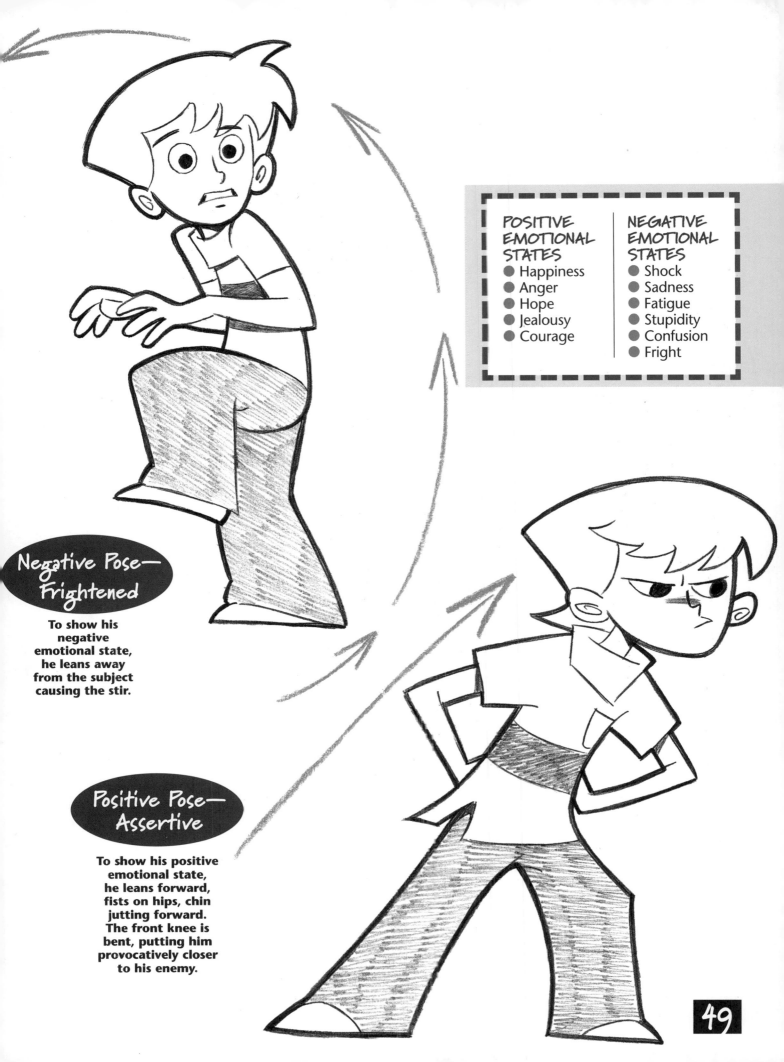

POSITIVE EMOTIONAL STATES
- Happiness
- Anger
- Hope
- Jealousy
- Courage

NEGATIVE EMOTIONAL STATES
- Shock
- Sadness
- Fatigue
- Stupidity
- Confusion
- Fright

Negative Pose— Frightened

To show his negative emotional state, he leans away from the subject causing the stir.

Positive Pose— Assertive

To show his positive emotional state, he leans forward, fists on hips, chin jutting forward. The front knee is bent, putting him provocatively closer to his enemy.

ARM MOVEMENTS

The *higher* you raise the arms in a pose, the more *emphatic* the pose becomes.

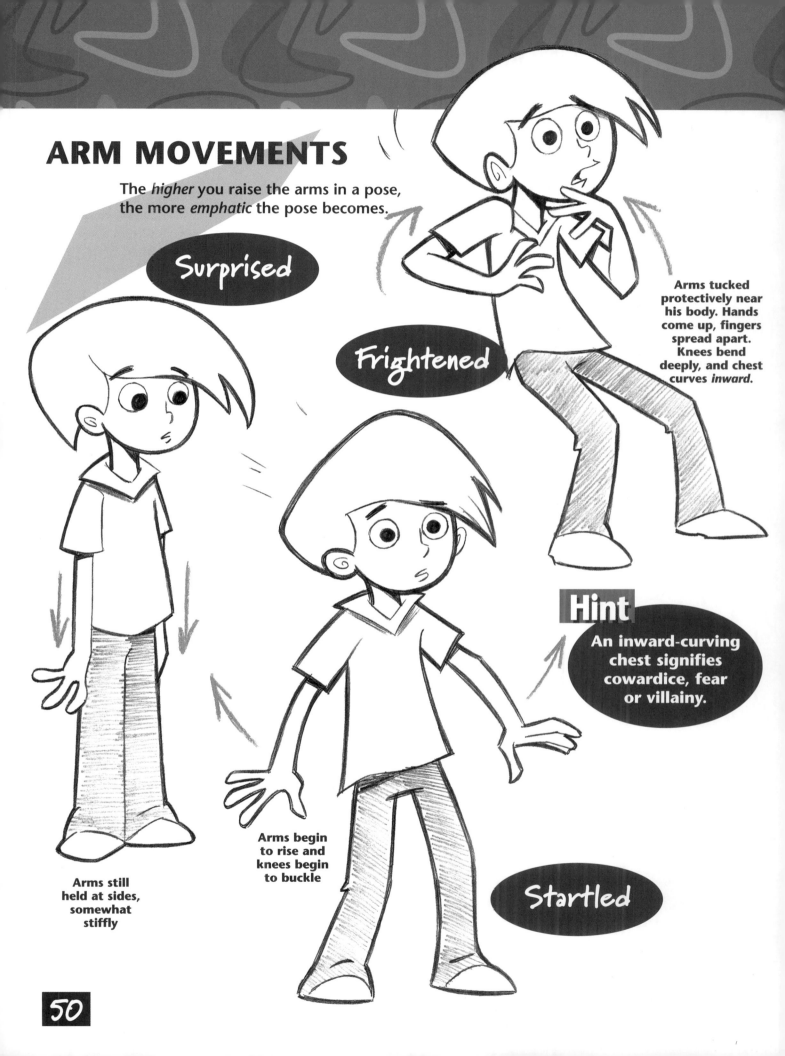

Surprised

Frightened

Startled

Arms tucked protectively near his body. Hands come up, fingers spread apart. Knees bend deeply, and chest curves *inward*.

Hint

An inward-curving chest signifies cowardice, fear or villainy.

Arms begin to rise and knees begin to buckle

Arms still held at sides, somewhat stiffly

RECLINING AND SITTING

The *longer* the distance between the toes and the head, the more relaxed the character will appear. Conversely, the *shorter* the distance between the toes and the head, the less relaxed she will look.

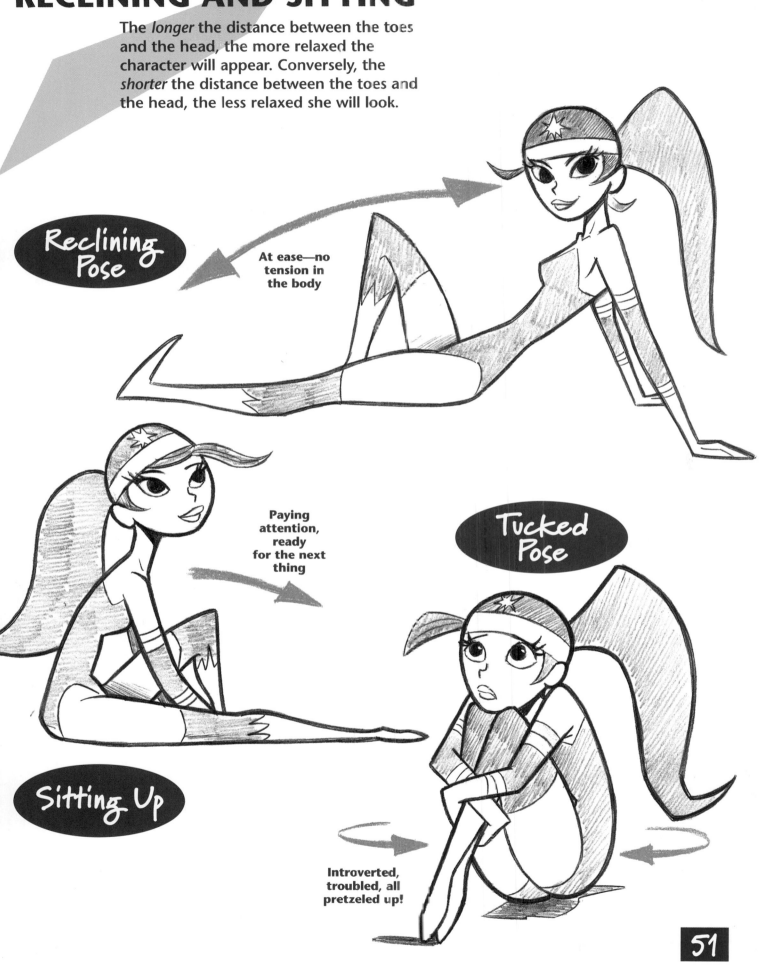

Reclining Pose

At ease—no tension in the body

Sitting Up

Paying attention, ready for the next thing

Tucked Pose

Introverted, troubled, all pretzeled up!

THE WOUNDED HERO

We love it when our heroes get knocked down, because it's so exciting to watch them struggle against the odds to get back up. And when they do, watch out! But just how do you want to show this? Did your hero merely take a light punch, or is he almost down for the count? It's all in the body language. Take a look.

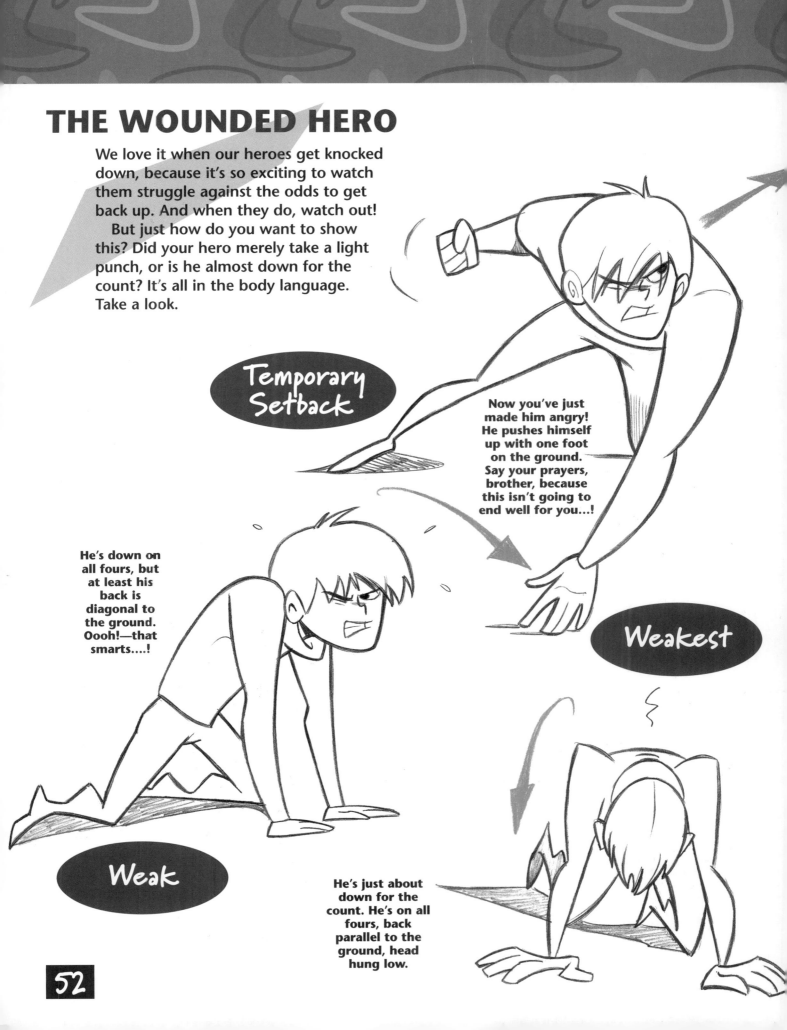

Temporary Setback

Now you've just made him angry! He pushes himself up with one foot on the ground. Say your prayers, brother, because this isn't going to end well for you...!

Weakest

He's down on all fours, but at least his back is diagonal to the ground. Oooh!—that smarts....!

Weak

He's just about down for the count. He's on all fours, back parallel to the ground, head hung low.

ANGER AND REVENGE

The same basic action, slightly tweaked, can make a pose read differently. And here's a good example of it. This big guy is having a friendly little chat with a slightly smaller action hero. Looks like the big fella is being fairly persuasive. So how dangerous is this situation for the meek character? Things get progressively more serious in this series of sketches, and the big guy's body language, particularly in his arms, shows this very clearly.

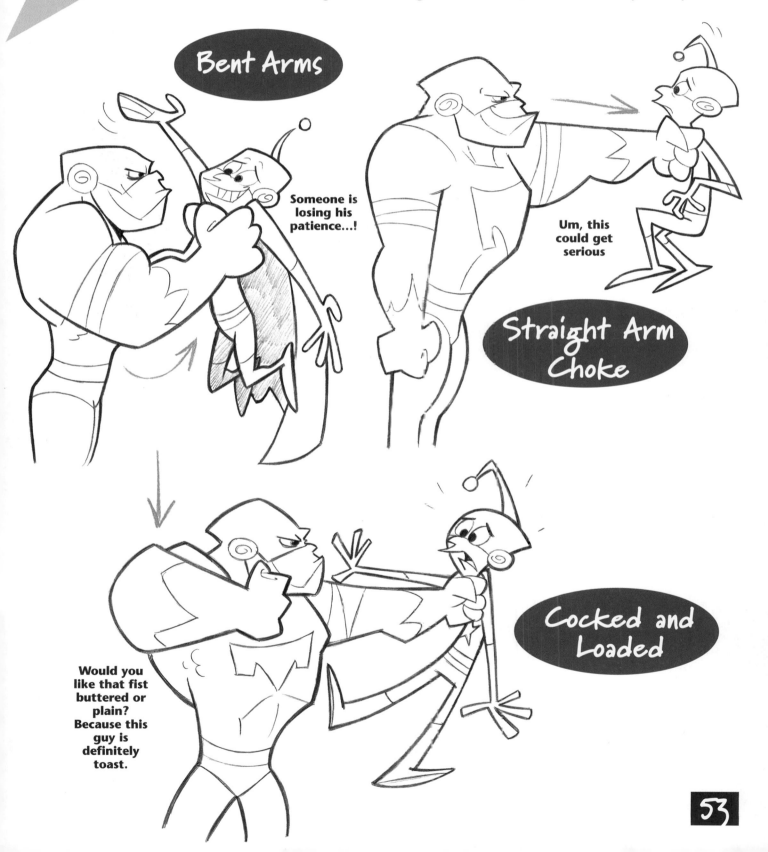

Bent Arms

Someone is losing his patience...!

Um, this could get serious

Straight Arm Choke

Cocked and Loaded

Would you like that fist buttered or plain? Because this guy is definitely toast.

THE ESSENTIAL ADVENTURE TRIO

The essential cartoon trio—the hero, his boss and his love interest—are perfect characters to practice on and apply the techniques you're learned so far. Whether you're reading comics or watching animated TV shows, you'll see them. They might be teenagers, kid detectives or grown-ups. But sooner or later, you're going to come across them: the harried journalist (he may be a columnist, TV anchor, editorial cartoonist, whatever), his girlfriend/co-worker, and their impatient boss.

Journalist Hero

PERSONALITY TRAITS
- Clean-cut
- Well built
- Angers when he smells evil
- Doesn't take offense easily
- Self-deprecating humor
- Loyal to a fault
- Lonely deep inside
- Unable to form meaningful attachments due to his need to maintain secret identity
- Has some sort of extra-human power, which he uses sparingly

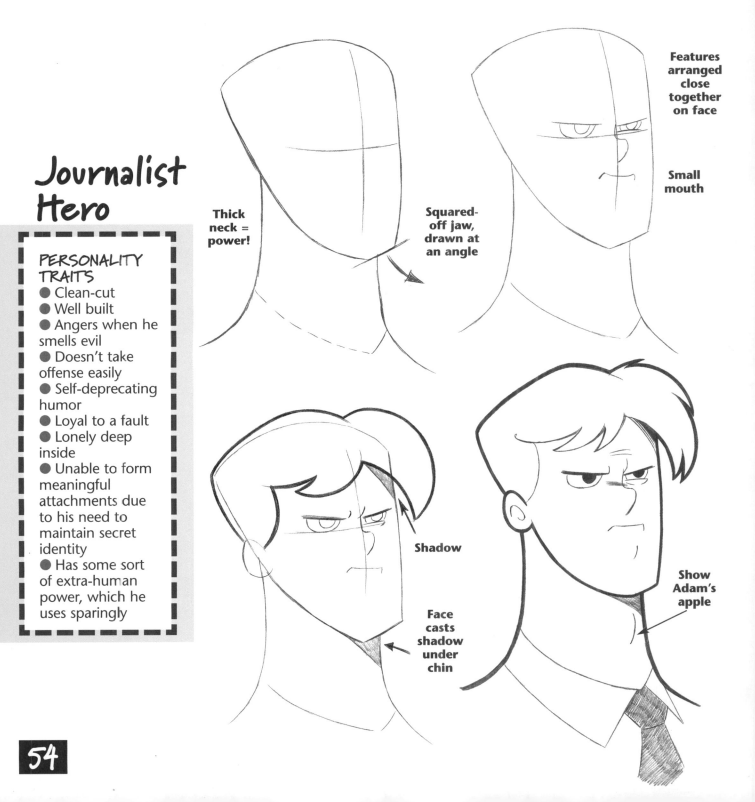

Features arranged close together on face

Small mouth

Thick neck = power!

Squared-off jaw, drawn at an angle

Shadow

Face casts shadow under chin

Show Adam's apple

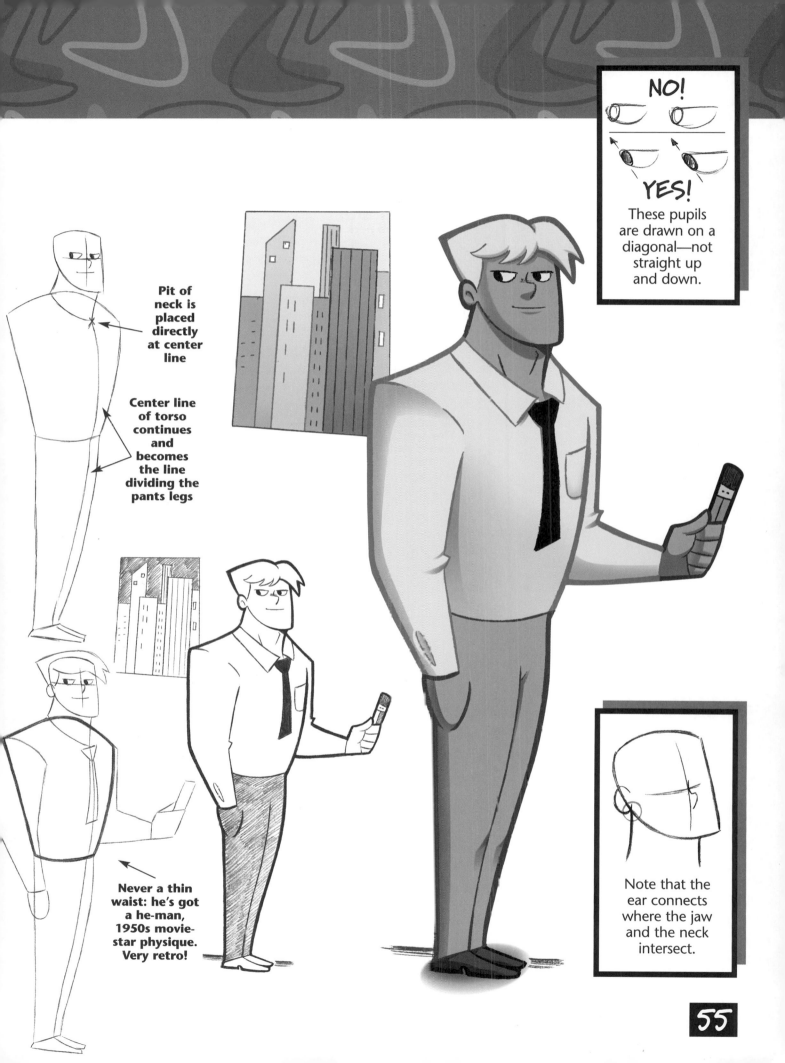

NO!

YES!

These pupils are drawn on a diagonal—not straight up and down.

Pit of neck is placed directly at center line

Center line of torso continues and becomes the line dividing the pants legs

Never a thin waist: he's got a he-man, 1950s movie-star physique. Very retro!

Note that the ear connects where the jaw and the neck intersect.

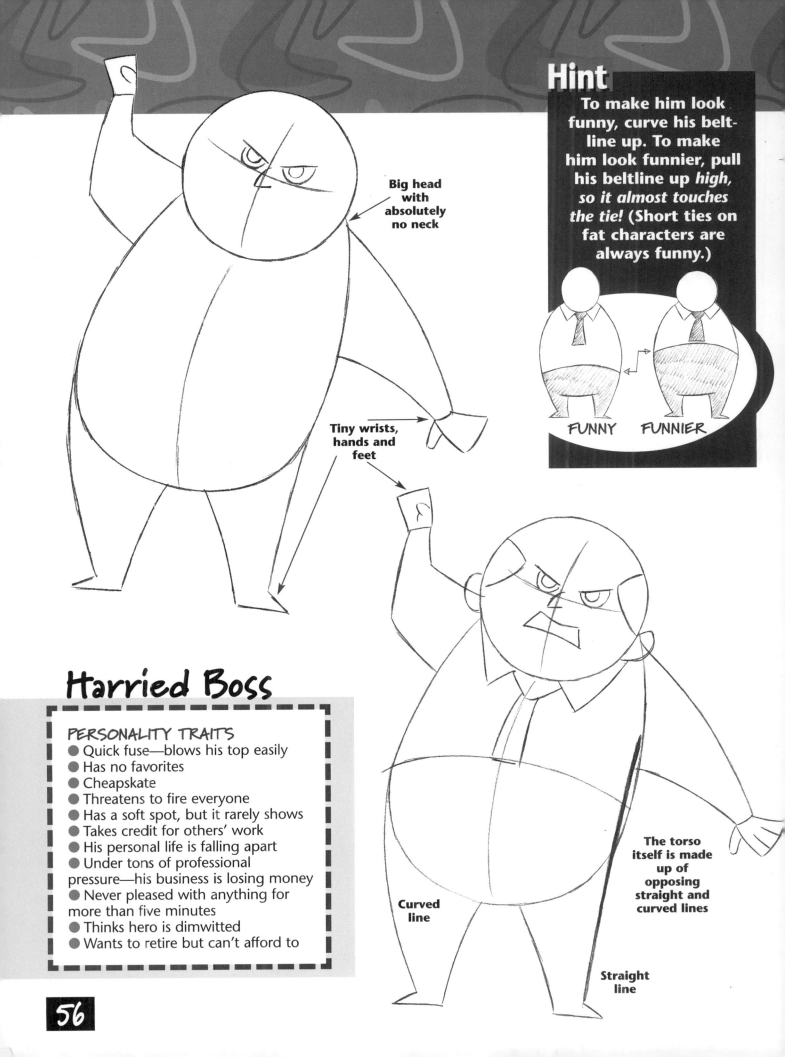

Big head with absolutely no neck

Hint

To make him look funny, curve his beltline up. To make him look funnier, pull his beltline up *high, so it almost touches the tie!* (Short ties on fat characters are always funny.)

FUNNY   FUNNIER

Tiny wrists, hands and feet

Harried Boss

PERSONALITY TRAITS
- Quick fuse—blows his top easily
- Has no favorites
- Cheapskate
- Threatens to fire everyone
- Has a soft spot, but it rarely shows
- Takes credit for others' work
- His personal life is falling apart
- Under tons of professional pressure—his business is losing money
- Never pleased with anything for more than five minutes
- Thinks hero is dimwitted
- Wants to retire but can't afford to

The torso itself is made up of opposing straight and curved lines

Curved line

Straight line

56

Pudgy arms, no elbows!

He's a stocky little fella. Make this come across by drawing his shoulders high, right up to his ears. And show absolutely no sign of a waistline at all. On tubby types, the tie creeps up the belly.

BITE HARD

Shadows appear at the corners of the mouth when the teeth are clenched!

When drawing newspapers, use rectangular blocks for photos and lines for text

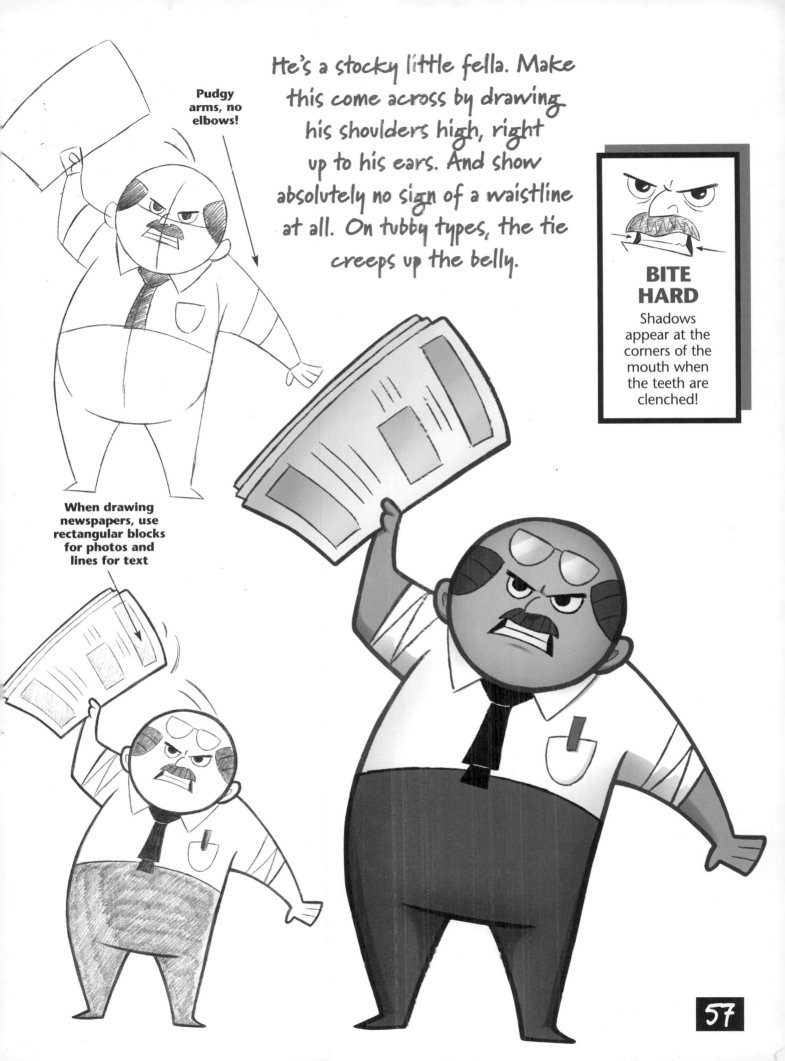

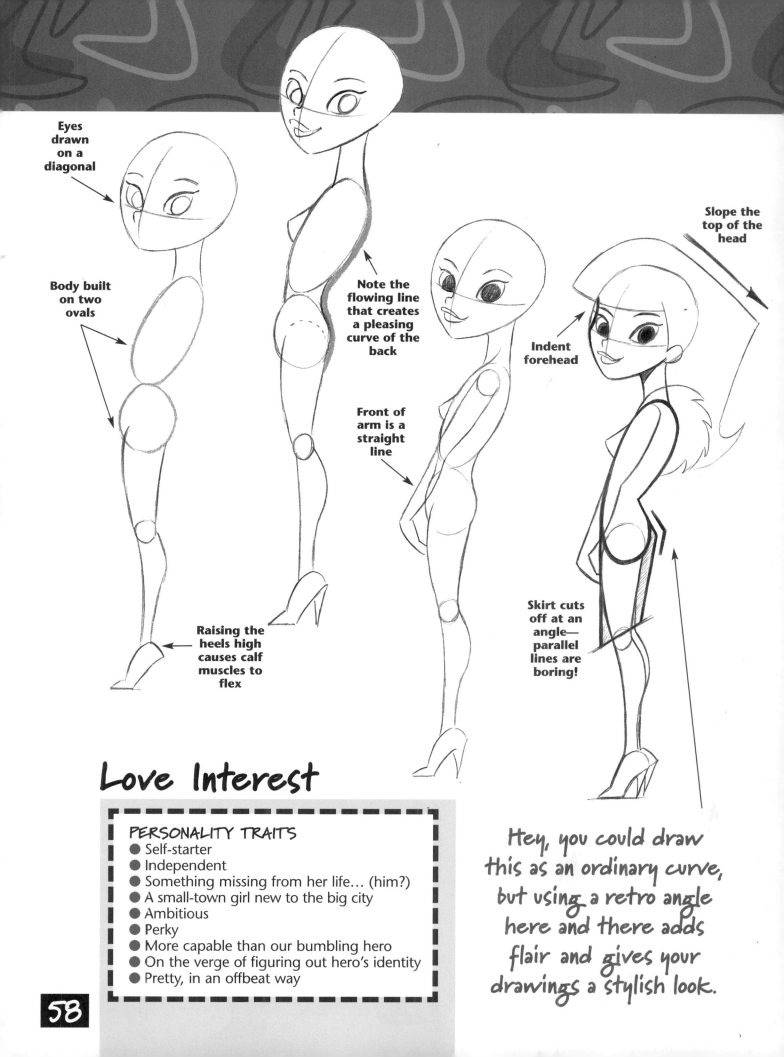

Eyes drawn on a diagonal

Body built on two ovals

Note the flowing line that creates a pleasing curve of the back

Front of arm is a straight line

Raising the heels high causes calf muscles to flex

Slope the top of the head

Indent forehead

Skirt cuts off at an angle—parallel lines are boring!

Love Interest

PERSONALITY TRAITS
- Self-starter
- Independent
- Something missing from her life… (him?)
- A small-town girl new to the big city
- Ambitious
- Perky
- More capable than our bumbling hero
- On the verge of figuring out hero's identity
- Pretty, in an offbeat way

Hey, you could draw this as an ordinary curve, but using a retro angle here and there adds flair and gives your drawings a stylish look.

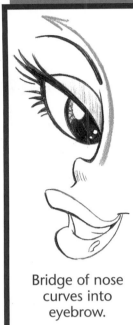

Bridge of nose curves into eyebrow.

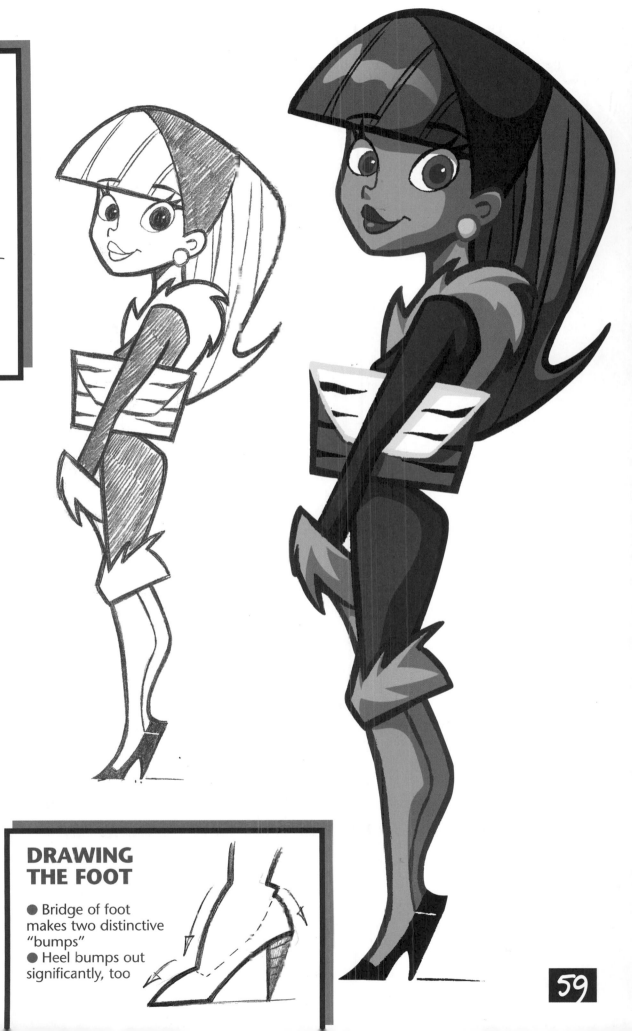

DRAWING THE FOOT

● Bridge of foot makes two distinctive "bumps"
● Heel bumps out significantly, too

EVIL, ROTTEN AND JUST PLAIN BAD GUYS

Our hero would be nowhere without the villains we all love to hate. Cartoon bad guys should always be portrayed with a tinge of humor. They're much more fun when they're *deliciously* evil, so show them enjoying their villainy. Sure, they want to make a billion bucks and take over the world. But they would be bad for free if they had to—that's how much they love their work.

Huge torso—built like a refrigerator!

Bottom of torso overhangs legs a bit

The Boss Man

Every good cartoon adventure needs a bad guy in charge—someone who's the brains of the outfit. The powerful bad guy is one of the most popular types. Notice how his smile just barely masks his ruthlessness.

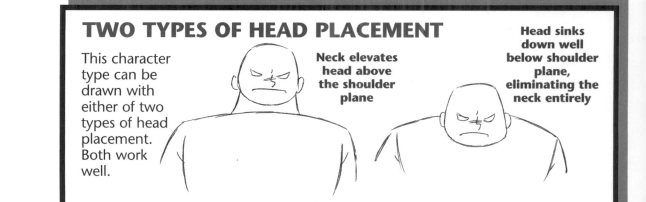

TWO TYPES OF HEAD PLACEMENT

This character type can be drawn with either of two types of head placement. Both work well.

Neck elevates head above the shoulder plane

Head sinks down well below shoulder plane, eliminating the neck entirely

Hint

The boss's chin is buried inside of his fat face (don't tell him I called him fat...!)

He's got a few henchmen to do his dirty work for him, though he is quite capable of brute force himself if the situation calls for it.

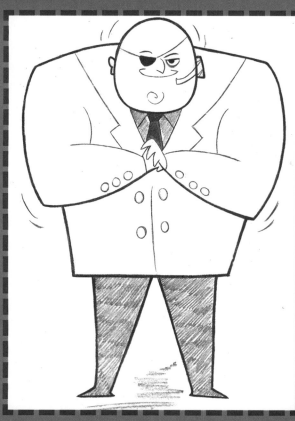

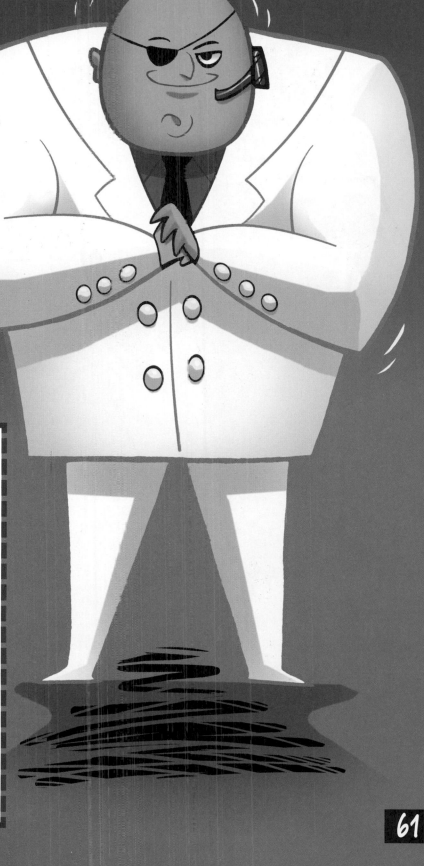

Elegant Evil—The Professor

The evil scientist is a classic bad guy. You'll find him mixing all sorts of ingredients to create a monstrous creature. Here, I've given him jackboots, a monocle and extremely erect posture—a sure sign of self-diagnosed superiority. Imagine him dangling our heroes over a vat of toxic goo.

Full Body

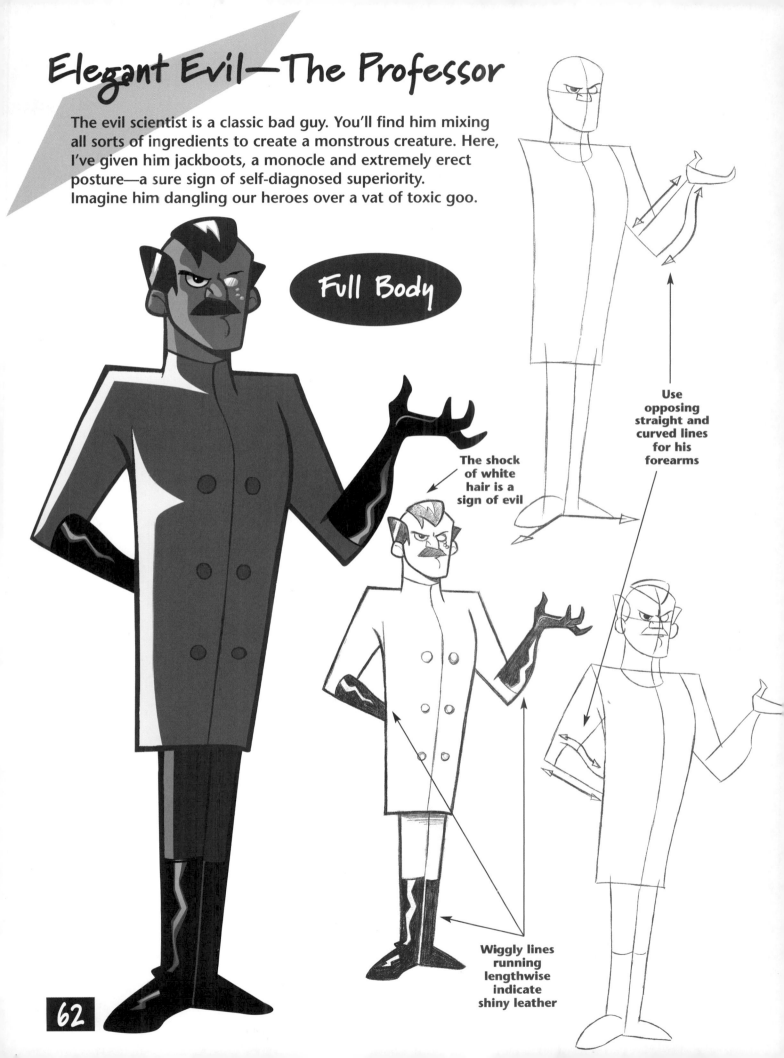

Use opposing straight and curved lines for his forearms

The shock of white hair is a sign of evil

Wiggly lines running lengthwise indicate shiny leather

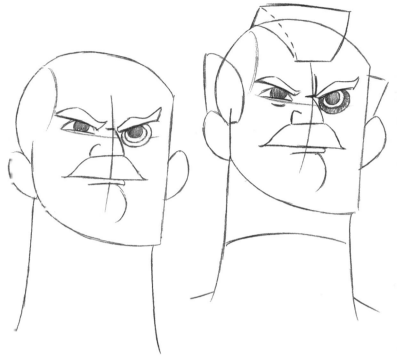

The Head

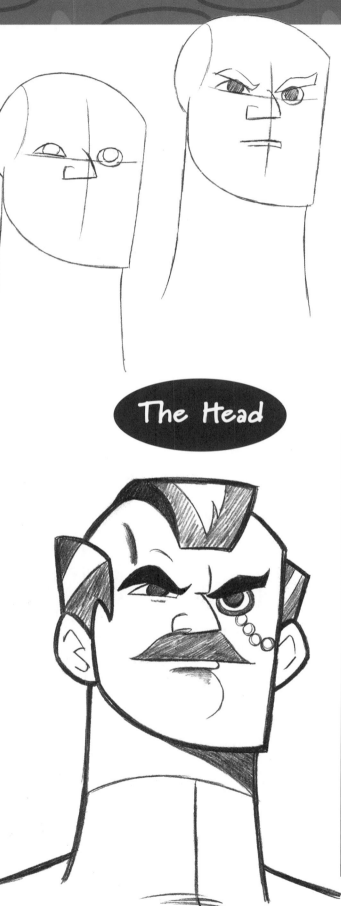

DRAWING THE MUSTACHE

A mustache that is drawn straight across the mouth horizontally eliminates the need for an upper lip. In fact, adding an upper lip below a mustache confuses the picture. You can, instead, cheat with the mustache: move it up and down slightly, like an upper lip, to make expressions, but not quite as elastically as an actual upper lip would.

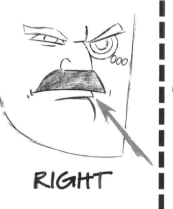

RIGHT

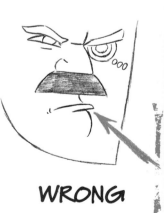

WRONG

This chapter is all about attitude—the emotion the character conveys through his or her pose. We'll focus on the details you need to communicate your character's attitude to the reader, and then we'll apply those details to spies and secret agents, too.

THE HEAD AND SHOULDERS

You don't always have to engage the entire body to convey your character's attitude. The head, neck and shoulders have all great power to communicate a wide range of feelings. They work as a unit. You can tense them, turn them, twist them or slump them.

How a Character Holds His Head

You can tell what a character thinks about himself merely by the way he holds his head.

HEAD HELD HIGH— SHOULDERS BACK	HEAD STRAIGHT— SHOULDERS NORMAL	HEAD DROOPING— SHOULDERS DROOPING
● Strong	● Polite	● Timid
● Brave	● Friendly	● Insecure
● Determined	● Good listener	● Disappointed
● Courageous	● Eager	● Mama's boy

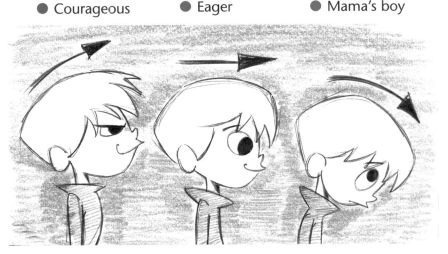

HEAD-SHOULDER COUNTERBALANCE

The head and shoulders naturally tilt in opposite directions: when the head tilts toward the right, the left shoulder tilts down (A).

When the head tilts to the left, the right shoulder tilts down (B).

When the head is straight, the shoulders are level, too (C).

Using this natural dynamic will prevent your drawings from looking stiff.

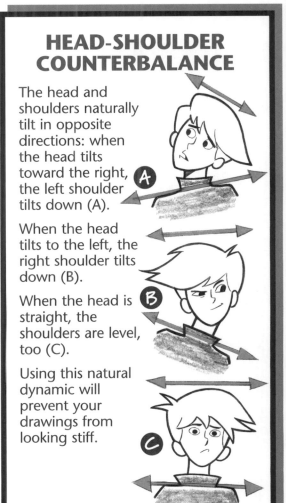

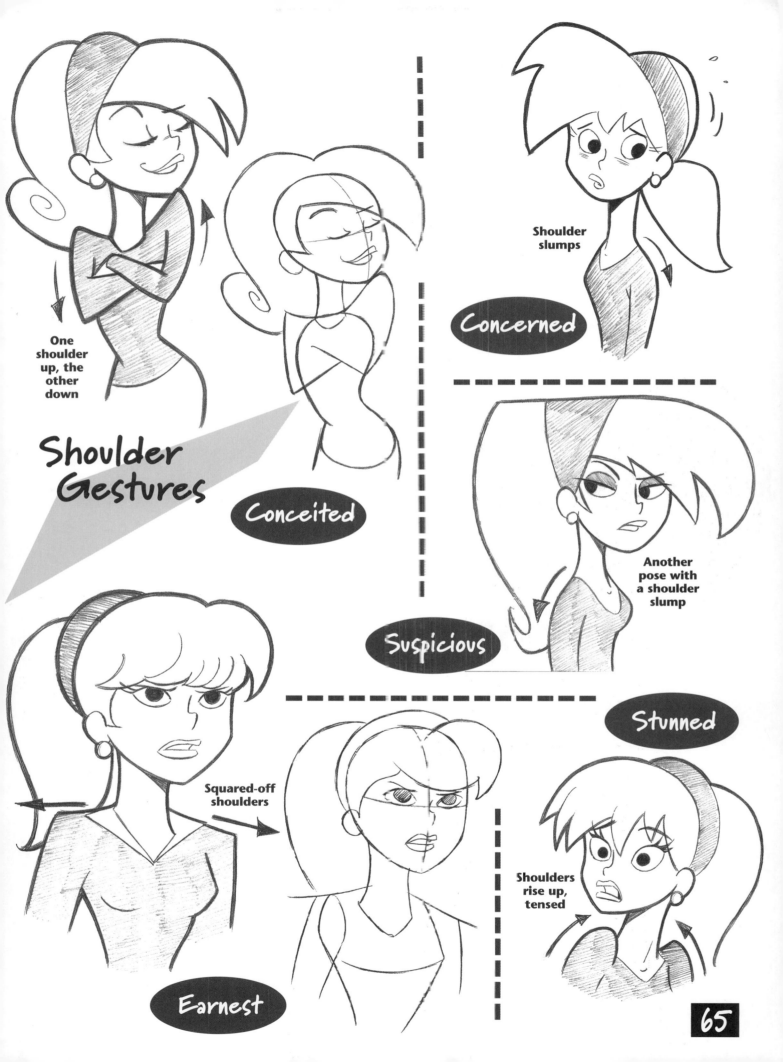

One shoulder up, the other down

Shoulder Gestures

Conceited

Concerned

Shoulder slumps

Another pose with a shoulder slump

Suspicious

Stunned

Squared-off shoulders

Shoulders rise up, tensed

Earnest

Adventure-Style Shoulders

When you draw shoulders realistically, you show that the collarbone goes straight across the top of the chest and the shoulders form two bumps on either end (A).

However, it's a sharper, adventure-style look to draw a single straight line all the way across the shoulders and collarbone, eliminating the shoulder bumps (B).

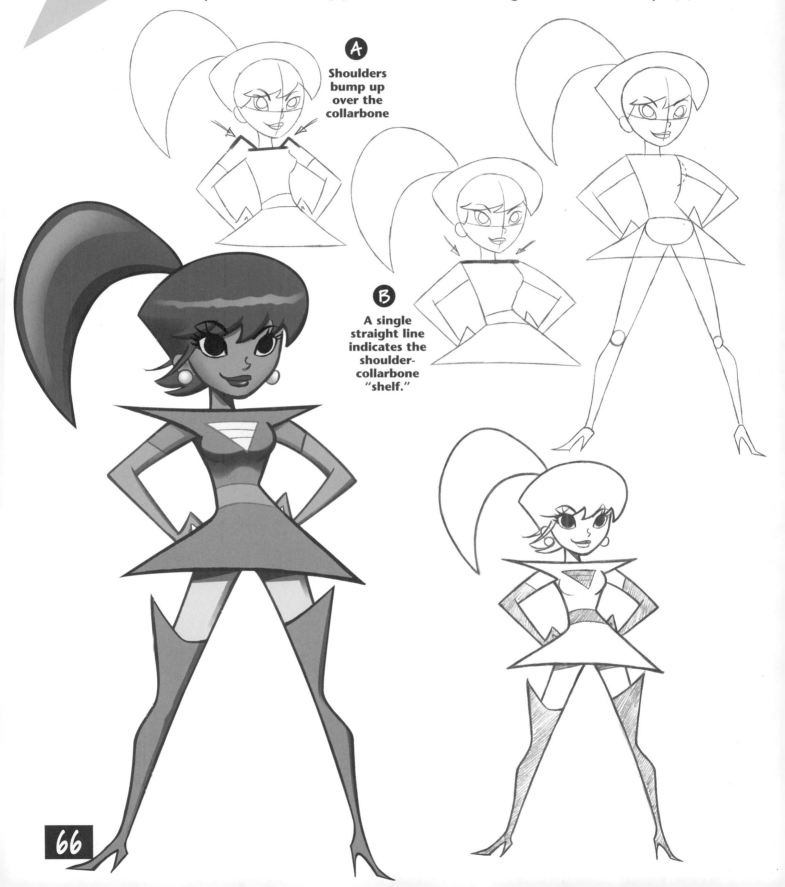

A

Shoulders bump up over the collarbone

B

A single straight line indicates the shoulder-collarbone "shelf."

DRAWING THE S-CURVE

Another technique for conveying body language rapidly is to use an S-curve. It gives the overall shape a pleasing flow. When you use an S-curve, make the body gently curve one way then slyly curve back in the other direction, without any sudden or sharp turns. *The S-curve should be a gentle, almost unnoticeable change of direction in the posture or pose.*

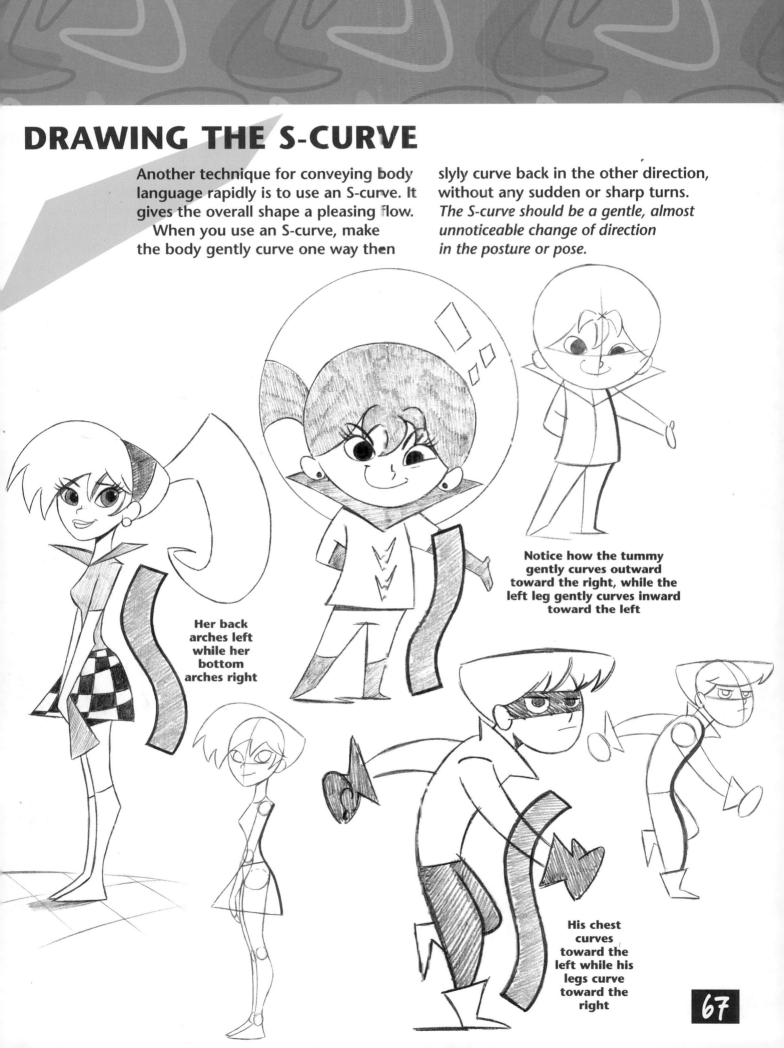

Notice how the tummy gently curves outward toward the right, while the left leg gently curves inward toward the left

Her back arches left while her bottom arches right

His chest curves toward the left while his legs curve toward the right

67

SHOULDER-HIP TILT

Boulders, cars and buses. To adventure heroes, they're all just playthings to toss and juggle. But if you draw your hero standing perfectly *erect* while balancing something gigantic on one side, it'll look awkward. The body has to **compensate** for a heavy weight by *tilting* the shoulder plane in one direction and the plane of the hips in the other. This is similar to the head and shoulder tilt we looked at earlier in this chapter—it's another way to give life and attitude to your characters.

Shoulders and hips tilt in *opposite* directions

AVOIDING SYMMETRY IN A POSE

While symmetry may not be the bogeyman of drawing that some make it out to be, if you can avoid it, it will probably make your pose stronger. How? By adding variety— and you do that by adding definition. Here's how: Something symmetrical has two sides that are the same. If you change one of the sides, you've added a new twist to the pose.

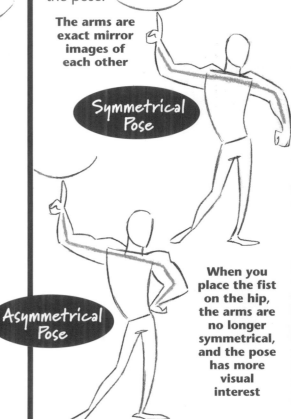

The arms are exact mirror images of each other

Symmetrical Pose

Asymmetrical Pose

When you place the fist on the hip, the arms are no longer symmetrical, and the pose has more visual interest

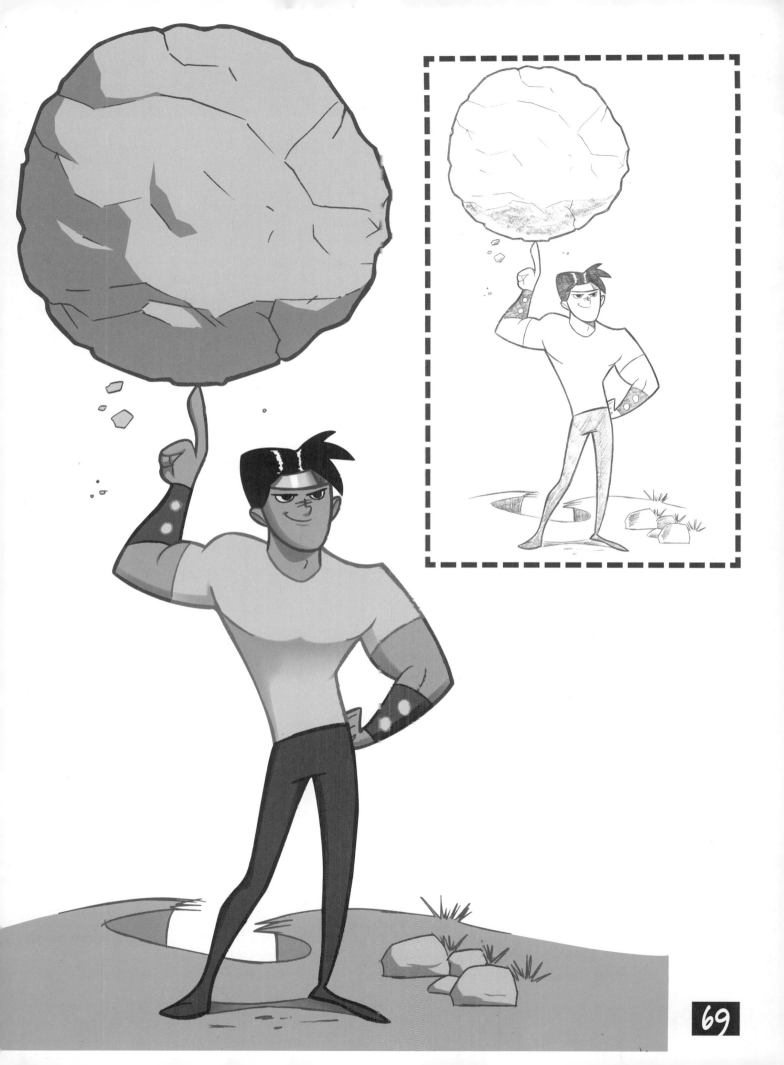

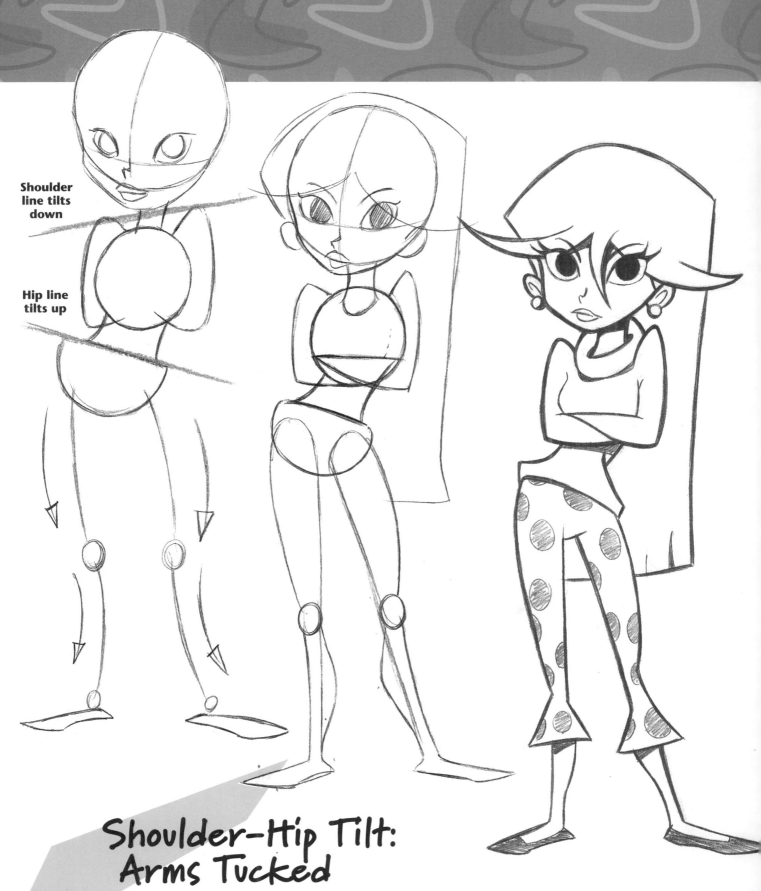

Shoulder line tilts down

Hip line tilts up

Shoulder-Hip Tilt: Arms Tucked

This classic pose emphasizes the tilt of the body and conveys impatience. Fold the arms and angle the hips and shoulders in opposite directions to make the *hips jut out* and the *shoulders pop up*, which is a decidedly *feminine look*.

WACKY RUN

The goofy run never fails to make me smile. It's so wonderfully silly to see this character, with her arms up over her head, leaning backward while running. To make her look even sillier, draw the hands **oversized**, with the fingers spread **way apart**, randomly flailing about.

The action line indicates the direction the character is leaning as she moves forward. She is not leaning in the direction she's moving...!

Foot pulls way back, which is a funny position

Normal run is effective, but not nearly as funny

WACKY-LOOKING HANDS

YES!

To draw wacky-looking hands, omit the thumb muscle and/or the palm heel. See how the palm heel and thumb muscle create a more normal, less silly-looking hand?

NO!

NO!

You can take all kinds of liberties with wacky characters—note how I floated the ponytail!

71

THE CLASSIC HERO-IN-DANGER POSE

Here's a character design that lets you put together everything you've learned in this chapter: the hero in distress. To draw this character, use the shoulder-hip tilt to turn a static pose into a dynamic one. Without the tilt, this guy would be standing up straight, as stiff as a board. But because I've tilted the hips and shoulders in opposite directions, the drawing has a dynamic feel. Try it in your drawings.

Weaker Pose

His shoulders are leaning into it, and that slight tilt of his head shows you that he's still got power to spare

Strong Pose

Hint

To draw funny superhero boots, draw the leg first, then draw the outline of the boot over it. You'll maintain the correct shape of the foot that way.

That head leaning back is a sign of fading fury! At this point, you might decide to bet on the wall!

Weakest Pose

Elbows in and knees in: uh-oh, that's a really bad sign. Anyone have a replacement hero handy?

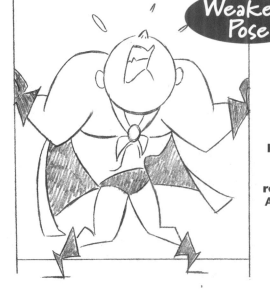

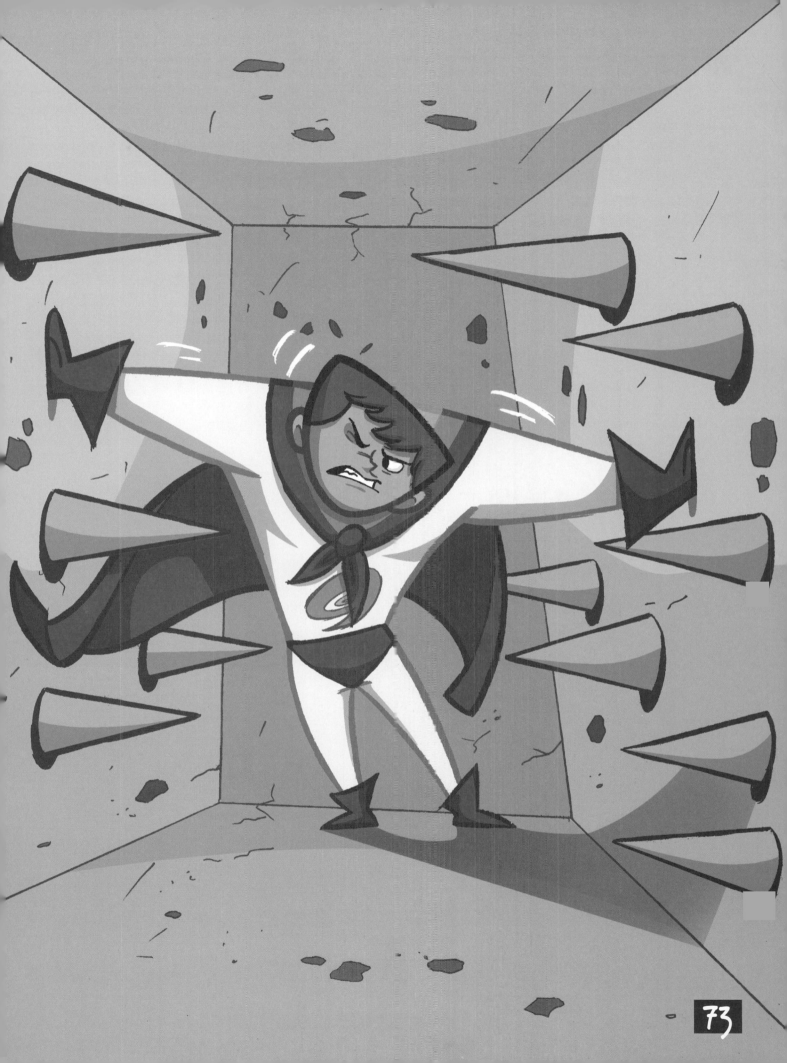

SPIES, SECRET AGENTS AND SABOTEURS

Another popular cast of characters in the adventure style is spies and their associates—secret agents, saboteurs, sneaky guys like that. These are cool characters, and there are three things you can highlight in order to make them look that way. The first is **costume**, the second is **pose**, and the third is **attitude**, which we've been learning about throughout this chapter.

Secret Agent

No matter who she's spying on, she looks great doing it! She's always in control of the situation, and, if she's got gadgets on her belt, that means she never runs out of high-tech tricks to get her and her friends out of a jam.

Hint

Note the different planes of the body at work to create this self-conscious pose.

Vertical plane

Diagonal— right

Diagonal— left

COSTUME She's dressed in black, to blend in with the night, and ready for anything—she's got all the right gear.

POSE She's self-consciously posed, as if staged by a choreographer, and totally in control.

ATTITUDE Is this job dangerous? Not to her—her attitude just drips with confidence.

Martial Arts Spy Guy

Get ready for flailing feet and fists! When you've got a group of bad guys who could use a little constructive criticism, send in a kung-fu expert. The secret to drawing this character is to suggest that his poses are more impressive than his actual moves!

COSTUME His costume instantly tells you who he is: a martial arts master.

POSE Cool, exotic fighting pose, with a great deal of movement.

ATTITUDE Notice the position of his hands and feet, as well as his facial expression. This guy means business.

ACTION LINE

The action line is a sketch line that indicates the general thrust or flow of the pose. Generally, the action line flows in the direction that the character's spine is moving (A).

When you have a pose with a lot of movement in it, such as this one, you may find it helpful to draw a second action line (B).

This figure really has two planes of movement, one for the arms and one for the entire body. This creates a dynamic impression.

A

B

Spy-Team Leader

Action heroes aren't the only ones who work in teams. Spies do, too. But each spy has his or her own specialty. For example:

● A person who can climb anything
● A master of disguise
● A techy-type communications specialist
● A mutant with special powers

Spies don't stay together through the entire story. They may have to infiltrate a well-guarded compound, for example, from many angles. One might be stationed on the roof while another monitors the progress from the high-tech van and a third makes his way inside dressed as a security officer, etc.

In a three-quarter rear view, we see most, but not all, of the back, so it's important to show some of the line of the spine

His face is youthful, but because he's a leader, he's got a more pronounced chin and angular jaw line than other teen characters.

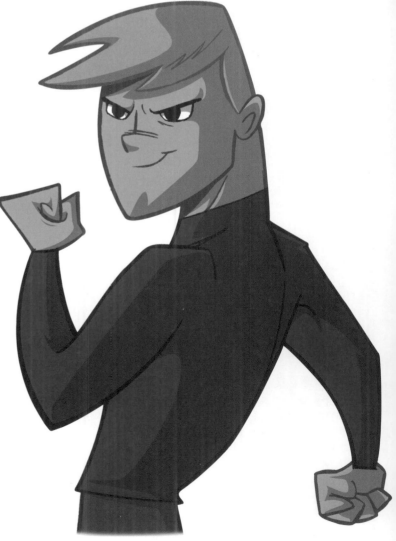

COSTUME Form-fitting turtleneck. Great for sneaking into tight spaces.

POSE His fist is raised, but not in a fighting pose—a classic sign of cartoon determination that says "Full steam ahead, gang!"

ATTITUDE His expression and body language show that he's a can-do type of guy. The bigger the challenge, the more he likes it!

Sci-Fi Spy

This character has a very retro look. A power belt, cool-looking bodysuit, trusty eye mask and space boots give her a sci-fi flair. She doesn't have to exist way off in the distant future. Cartoon sci-fi is here and now—all it takes is an evil scientist with a giant robot programmed to take over the world and a hero with a ponytail who is determined to stop him!

The head is a large circle. It's a very simple shape, which gives it a retro look.

The shoulders are straight across, but not very wide

The torso is the shape of an elongated pear—can you see that?

COSTUME This character sports a space-suit-type uniform, but without the extravagant technogear.

POSE Just because she's a spy doesn't mean she can't be humorous. Here, she's losing patience—perhaps her partner can't crack the code to open that high-security door.

ATTITUDE Her body language tells you that she's the know-it-all of the group.

BENDING THE TORSO

The torso is flexible and can twist and bend forward as well as backward. Either way, be sure it retains its hourglass shape.

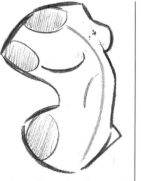

Bending backward | **Neutral** | **Bending forward**

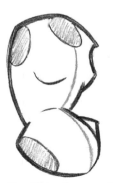

UNDERSIDE OF CHIN
Add the shadow under the chin to show that you are viewing the character from below (take a look at the bottom of the cube).

THE SECRET SERVICE AGENT

He's nameless and expressionless, and his eyes are hidden beneath dark, dark lenses. What does he see? *Everything.* That's because he's a Secret Service agent. His deadpan expression and one-track mind make him fun to draw. Since this character is in the business of observing everyone, we draw him from the vantage point of us observing him! To do that, we either have to *look up at him at an angle,* or *look down at him at an angle.*

THE UP ANGLE

Look at the difference between an object viewed from below and an object viewed from the side (normal view, or neutral angle).

NEUTRAL ANGLE
This cube is drawn at a neutral angle, neither up nor down. As a result you can't see the top or the bottom of the cube.

UP ANGLE
In the up angle, we see the bottom of the cube.

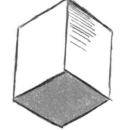

DIMINISHING PERSPECTIVE
Here we're also seeing the cube from the bottom, but because of perspective, it looks as though it's getting smaller toward the top.

Cartoonists always color secret service agents in dark clothing, to poke fun at their mirthless, self-important manner.

This guy sees a conspiracy when his order of French fries arrives 30 seconds late.

79

The Down Angle

When you draw a character from the down angle, your readers feel like they're situated above the character, looking down on him or her.

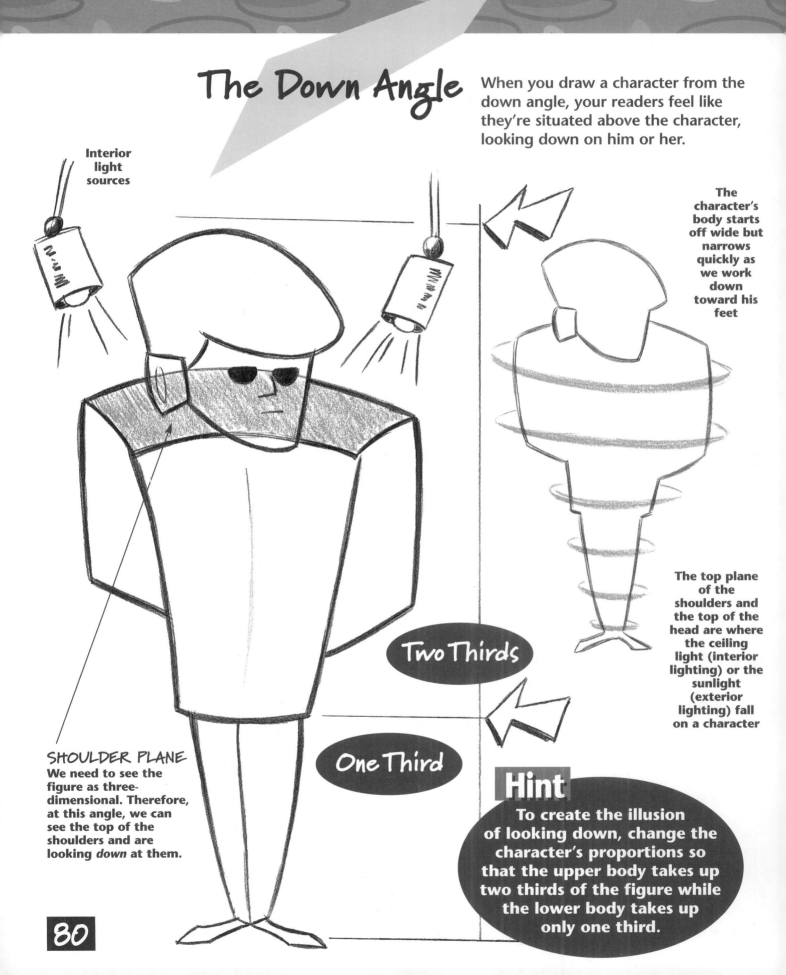

Interior light sources

The character's body starts off wide but narrows quickly as we work down toward his feet

The top plane of the shoulders and the top of the head are where the ceiling light (interior lighting) or the sunlight (exterior lighting) fall on a character

Two Thirds

One Third

SHOULDER PLANE
We need to see the figure as three-dimensional. Therefore, at this angle, we can see the top of the shoulders and are looking *down* at them.

Hint
To create the illusion of looking down, change the character's proportions so that the upper body takes up two thirds of the figure while the lower body takes up only one third.

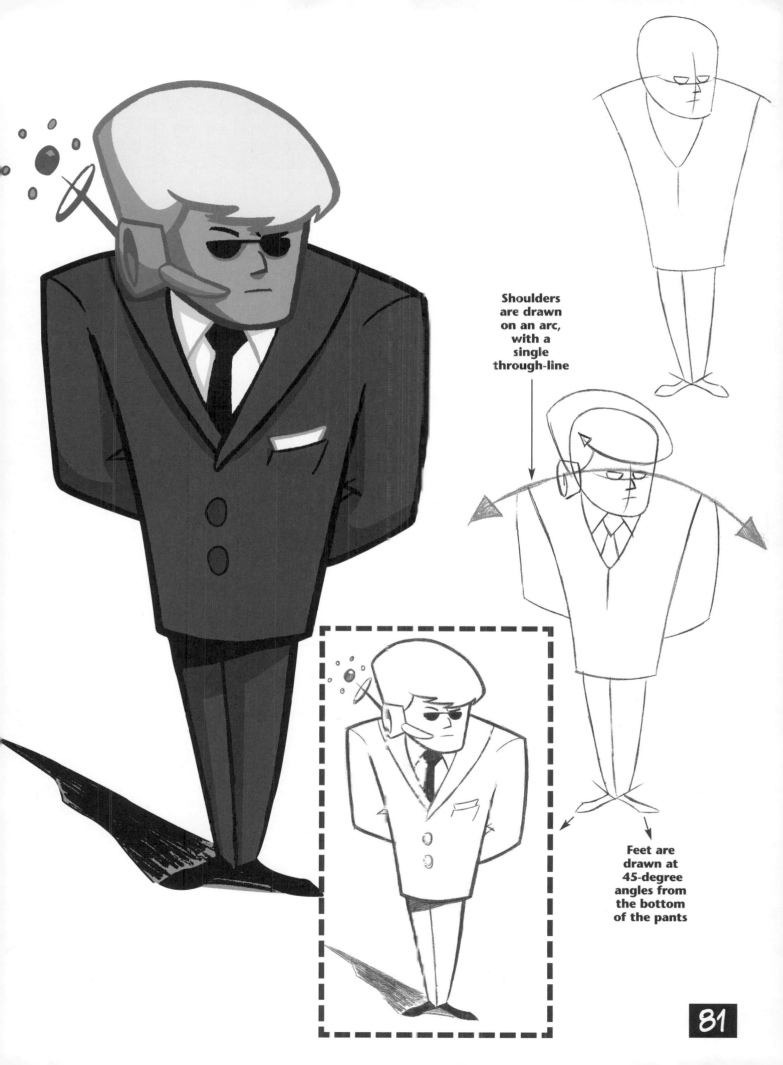

Shoulders are drawn on an arc, with a single through-line

Feet are drawn at 45-degree angles from the bottom of the pants

ACTION! PUTTING CHARACTERS IN MOTION

THE BIG PICTURE

Oftentimes, you see a drawing, like it and try to copy it, following the lines but ending up with vastly different results. Why? Because you're following the details but missing the big picture.

For example, you could watch a pitcher and try to imitate his movements, but unless you knew if he was throwing a curve or a fastball, you wouldn't do a very good job of copying

him. For the same reason, whenever you draw complicated poses or motions, you need to know the big picture—the end result of the character's action. To know that, you need to be able to deconstruct the pose, to break it down into its most important parts. That's what I'll show you in this chapter.

Let's start by deconstructing a fairly goofy super-action guy.

Direction of the Torso

Here's a sci-fi soldier character, a big, burly guy. Notice that the body stretches in different directions. This is important for creating a feeling of motion. The torso (A) veers off to the right, while the chest (B)

makes a sharp angle back toward the left. The basic formula for drawing him is: *huge* upper body and *tiny* legs. And don't underestimate the width of the shoulders. You can't make them too big!

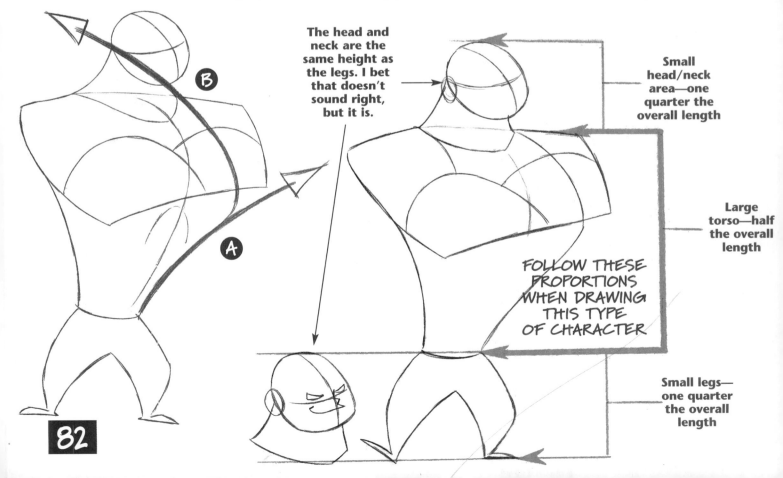

B

The head and neck are the same height as the legs. I bet that doesn't sound right, but it is.

A

Small head/neck area—one quarter the overall length

Large torso—half the overall length

FOLLOW THESE PROPORTIONS WHEN DRAWING THIS TYPE OF CHARACTER

Small legs—one quarter the overall length

Repeating the logo design helps to create an identity for the character through his costume—a big, fat zero!

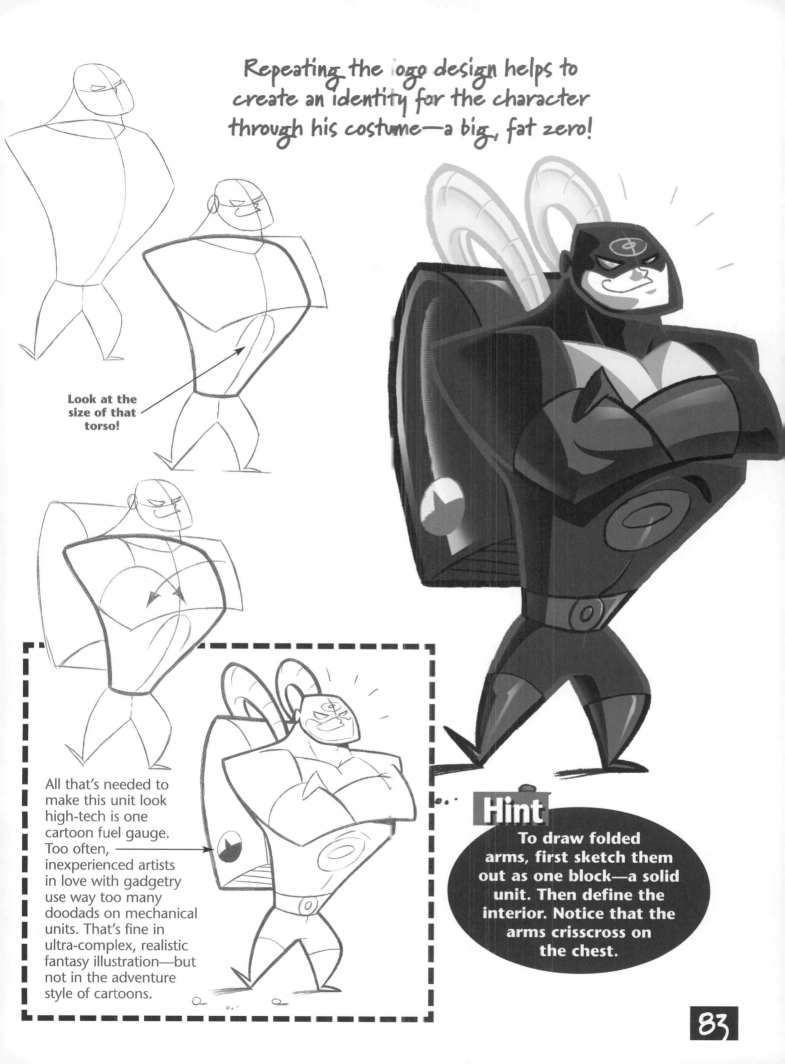

Look at the size of that torso!

All that's needed to make this unit look high-tech is one cartoon fuel gauge. Too often, inexperienced artists in love with gadgetry use way too many doodads on mechanical units. That's fine in ultra-complex, realistic fantasy illustration—but not in the adventure style of cartoons.

Hint

To draw folded arms, first sketch them out as one block—a solid unit. Then define the interior. Notice that the arms crisscross on the chest.

ACTION POSES

Drawing action in adventure-style cartoons is all about conspicuous posing. It's really a **caricature** of action rather than the realistic representation of action. So sprinkle in a healthy dose of humor, either by exaggerating the motion or by making it look super-easy or super-difficult.

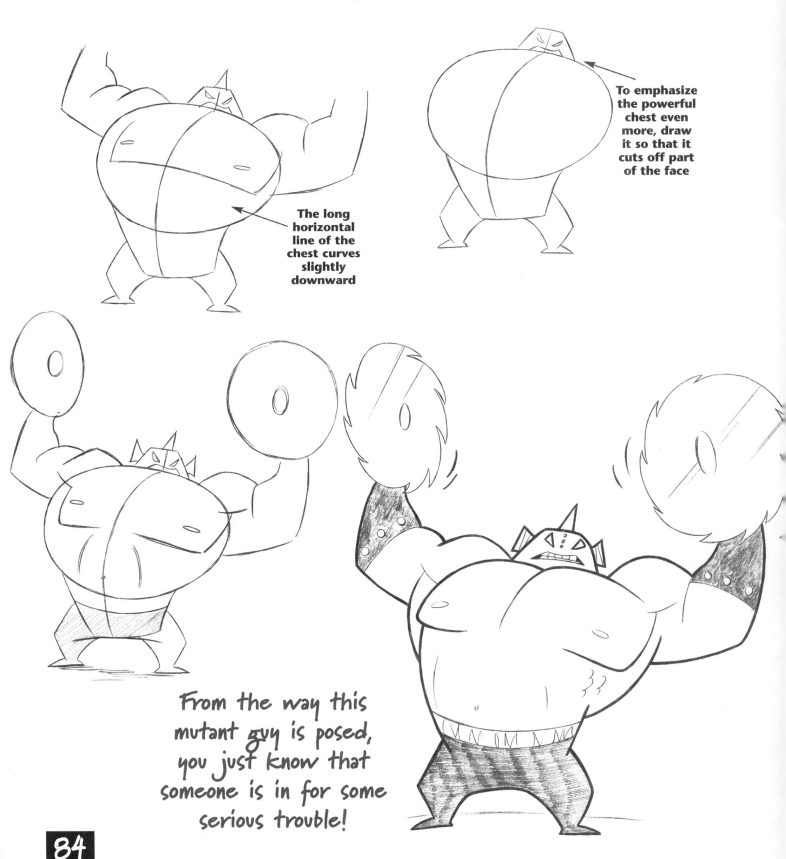

To emphasize the powerful chest even more, draw it so that it cuts off part of the face

The long horizontal line of the chest curves slightly downward

From the way this mutant guy is posed, you just know that someone is in for some serious trouble!

CHARACTERS IN MOTION

The following pages show you how to add attitude and action to your heroes and villains.

Let's start with the swinger on this page. Where is this guy going? I could have just drawn him swinging to the side but instead, I drew him swinging out of control and straight toward the viewer! A little attitude adds a lot of humor to an action pose.

Ready or Not, Here I Come!

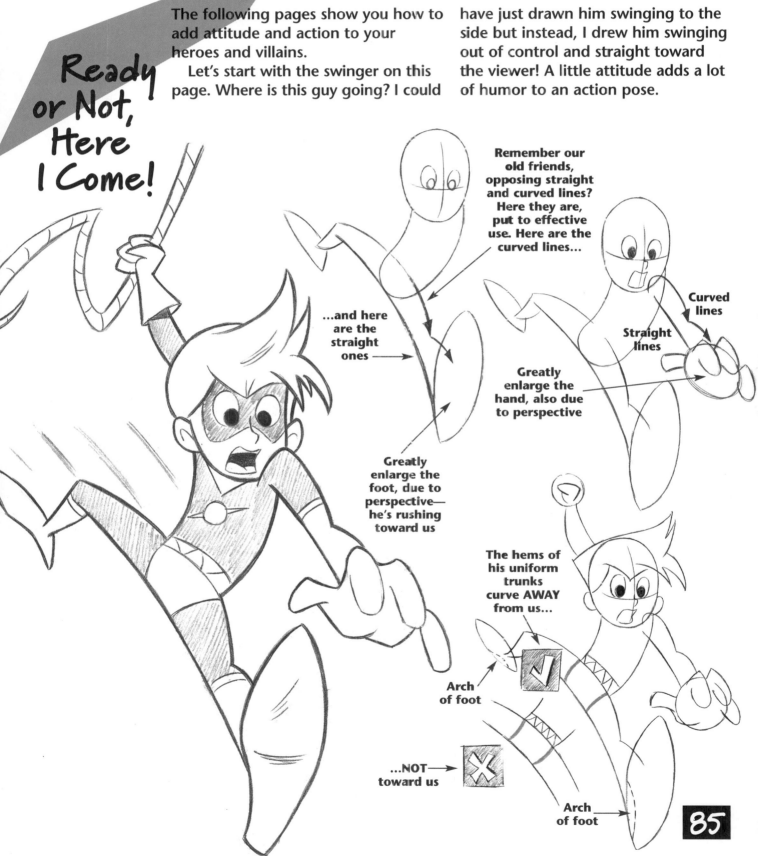

Remember our old friends, opposing straight and curved lines? Here they are, put to effective use. Here are the curved lines...

...and here are the straight ones

Curved lines

Straight lines

Greatly enlarge the hand, also due to perspective

Greatly enlarge the foot, due to perspective—he's rushing toward us

The hems of his uniform trunks curve AWAY from us...

Arch of foot

...NOT toward us

Arch of foot

Moving in an Arc

Newton—the scientist, not the cookie—might have proved that objects in motion tends to move in straight lines, but in cartoons, things tend to move in arcs. So, draw your character swinging up, down or diagonally. As for going sideways across the page, not so interesting.

Hint

An over-the-top pose like this allows you to caricature the action and adds to the comic effect. In this case, it's the character's femininity that's exaggerated.

Point the toes. Don't pull them back.

Again, the toes are pointed, not pulled back

Don't Make Me Use This!

Here's a version of the classic Finger Energy Beam. Note that I've drawn a controlled attack rather than an all-out assault. It's just plain funnier this way.

If you were to show him really leaning into the pose, that beam of energy would appear anticlimactic—because he's a weak character. So instead, we go in the other direction: we downplay the action. He's standing pretty much straight up and down, just hovering above the ground—all he's doing is giving a little jab with his finger at his enemy and letting a few sparks fly.

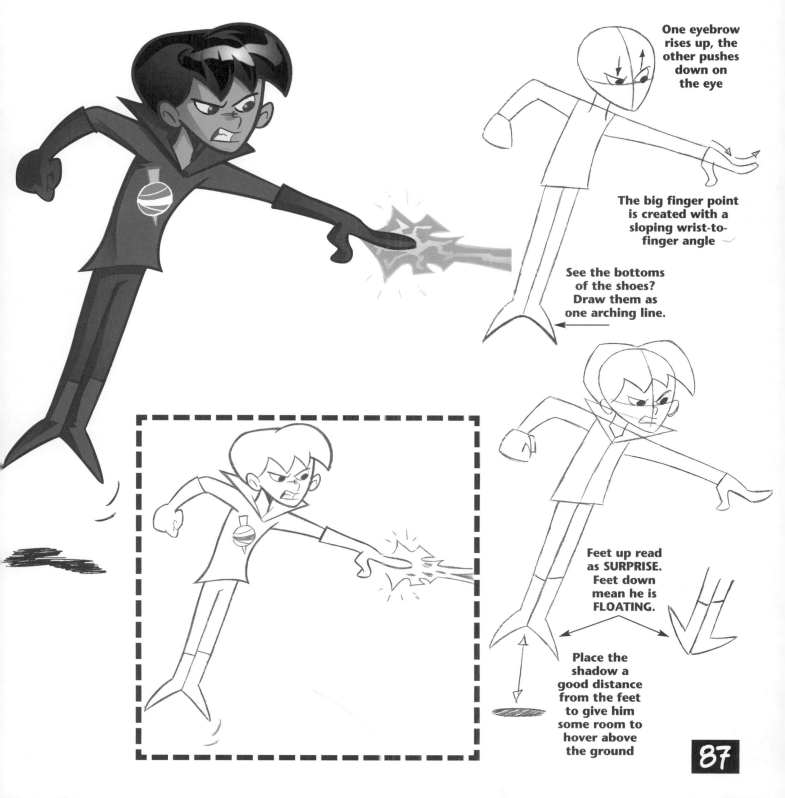

One eyebrow rises up, the other pushes down on the eye

The big finger point is created with a sloping wrist-to-finger angle

See the bottoms of the shoes? Draw them as one arching line.

Feet up read as SURPRISE. Feet down mean he is FLOATING.

Place the shadow a good distance from the feet to give him some room to hover above the ground

PUNCH LIKE YOU WALK!

In adventure-style cartoons, there is only one punch: the big windup, KA-POW puncharoo. It's the punch that sends the evil guy through a wall of bricks, and straight into the clink. This is where we pull out all the stops and use as much motion as possible.

There are a variety of climactic punches, and each one has its own particular look and use. I'll show you how to draw all of them, each on a different,

cool character, naturally! But first, let's look at the basic mechanics of the punch.

Notice that when a person walks, he moves the limbs on the same side of his body in *opposite* directions: right leg forward, right arm back; left leg forward, left arm back.

A character punches in exactly the same way: left arm forward, left leg back. The difference is that when punching, the character leans **way into the pose**.

Opposite legs and arms swing forward and back. Body is upright, and front leg is straight.

Walking

Hint

SPEED LINES are essential to the punch—they indicate action and show the path of the punch. By identifying the origin of the punch, the speed lines make the swing look BIGGER.

Opposite legs and arms move forward and back. Body leans forward. FRONT KNEE BENDS WAY DOWN, AND BACK LEG GOES WAY UP IN THE AIR.

Punching

FIGHT-ENDING, BAD-GUY-CLOBBERING PUNCHES

Punching Up Diagonally

Diagonals—not love—are what make the cartoon world go 'round. They're so much more exciting than horizontal lines. Look at the action you get from them. And it's not just the punching arm itself—the diagonal extends all the way through to the other arm, creating one huge diagonal across the page.

This is the punch your character uses to launch his enemy into orbit with a final, powerful blow. It's lights out for the bad guy.

Knee dips close to the ground: the lower the knee, the more forceful the punch

Main force

One continuous diagonal across the shoulders

Minor force

89

Punching Down Diagonally

This is your go-to punch for all types of fight scenes. It's an excellent action move—maybe not the fight-ending punch, but one sure to send bad guys reeling and give the good guy time to regain the upper hand.

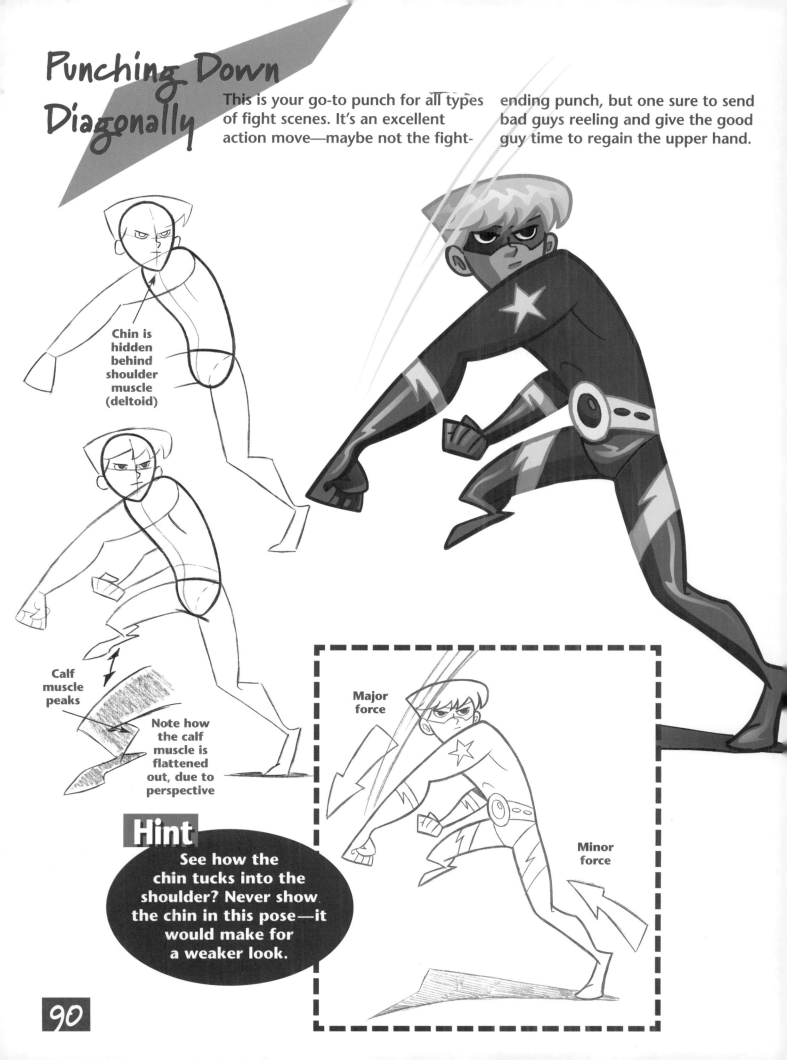

Chin is hidden behind shoulder muscle (deltoid)

Calf muscle peaks

Note how the calf muscle is flattened out, due to perspective

Hint

See how the chin tucks into the shoulder? Never show the chin in this pose—it would make for a weaker look.

Major force

Minor force

The Hammer Fist

With absolutely zero effort and no movement in the rest of his body, a thug lowers the ka-boom on top of his opponent's head, driving the poor guy into the ground like a nail into a wooden plank. To top things off, give your thug a casual, even bored, expression.

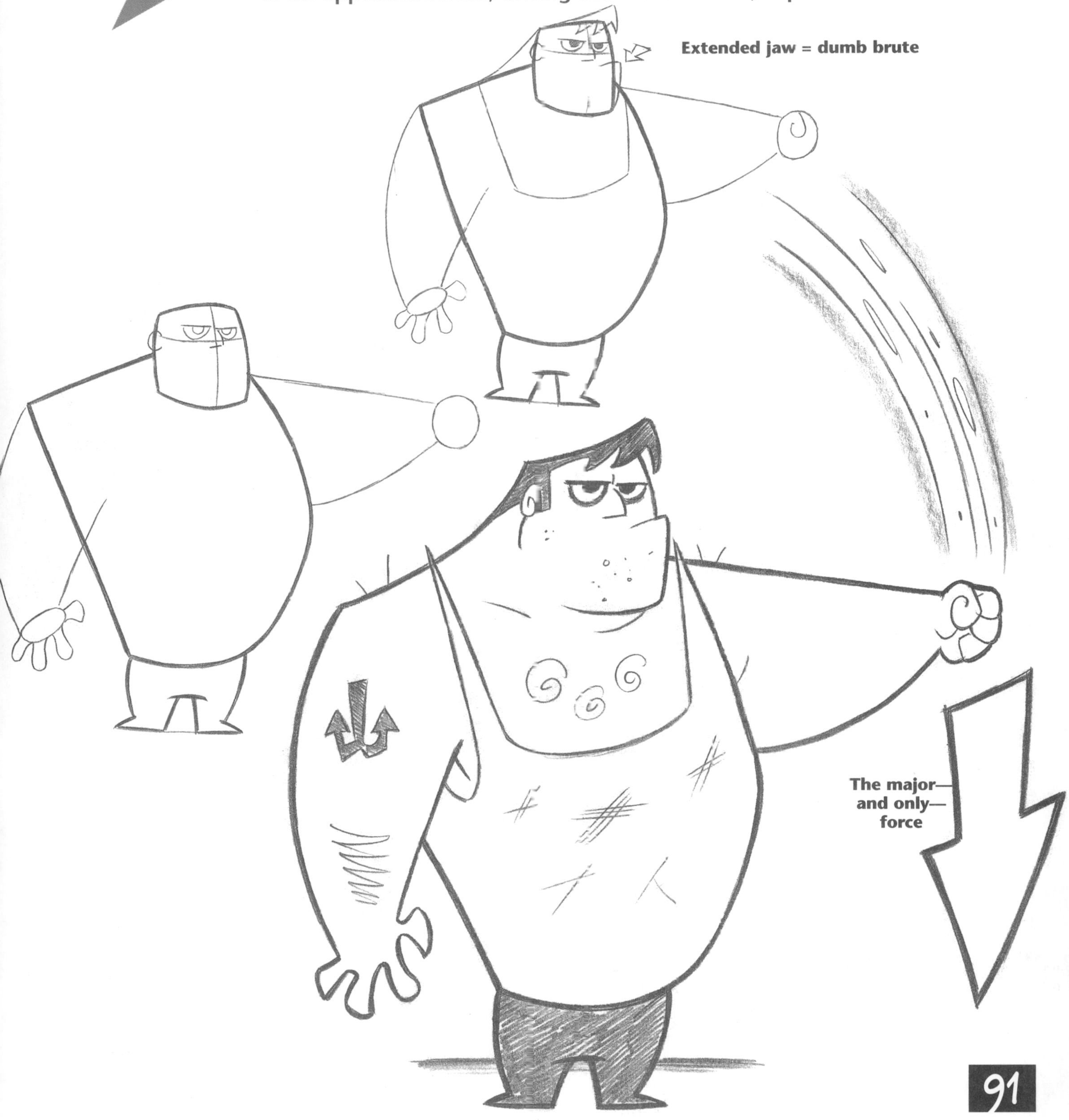

Extended jaw = dumb brute

The major—and only—force

Windmill Punch

Another humorous punch is the windmill, which comes from below and semicircles up over the head. It's another knockout device, used to finish off a diabolical enemy. Notice how the punch travels along an arc, as indicated by the speed lines. Both arms fan out, sort of like a windmill.

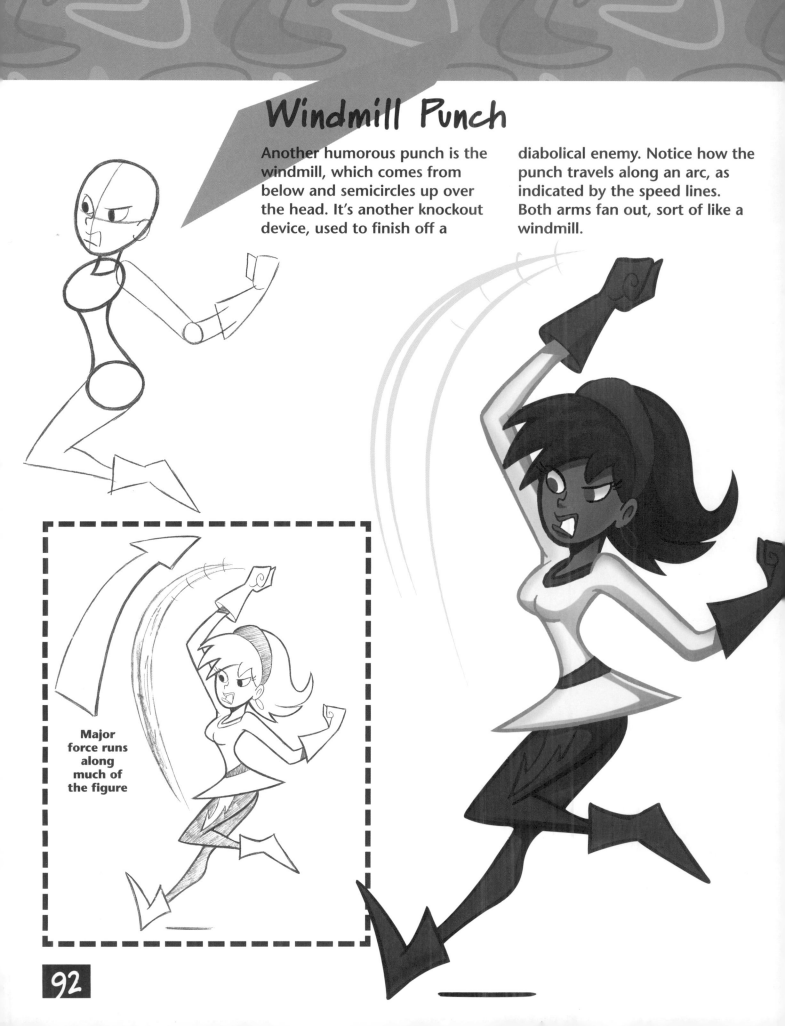

Major force runs along much of the figure

Hooking Punch

This is the one exception to the "Big Punch" rule. If your characters are close together— for example, in tight quarters—then there's no room for a huge windup and follow-through. But you can still squeeze in a hooking punch.

Upper arm overlaps the forearm

Upper arm is out in front

Speed line swirls around the character, giving the illusion of traveling sideways

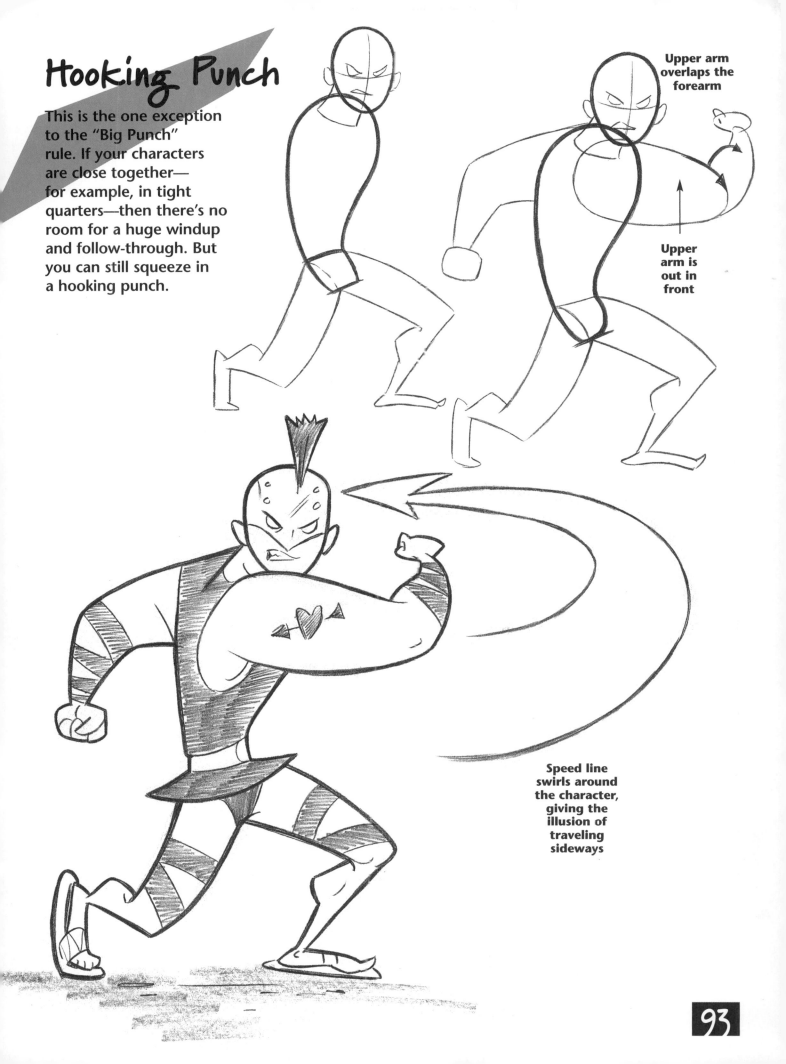

Running Punch

Fed up with the bad guy's shenanigans? Give him a running punch—the punch your hero uses when he just isn't gonna take it anymore. Maybe your hero's been knocked down one too many times. This time, when he picks himself up, he's mad, and he means business.

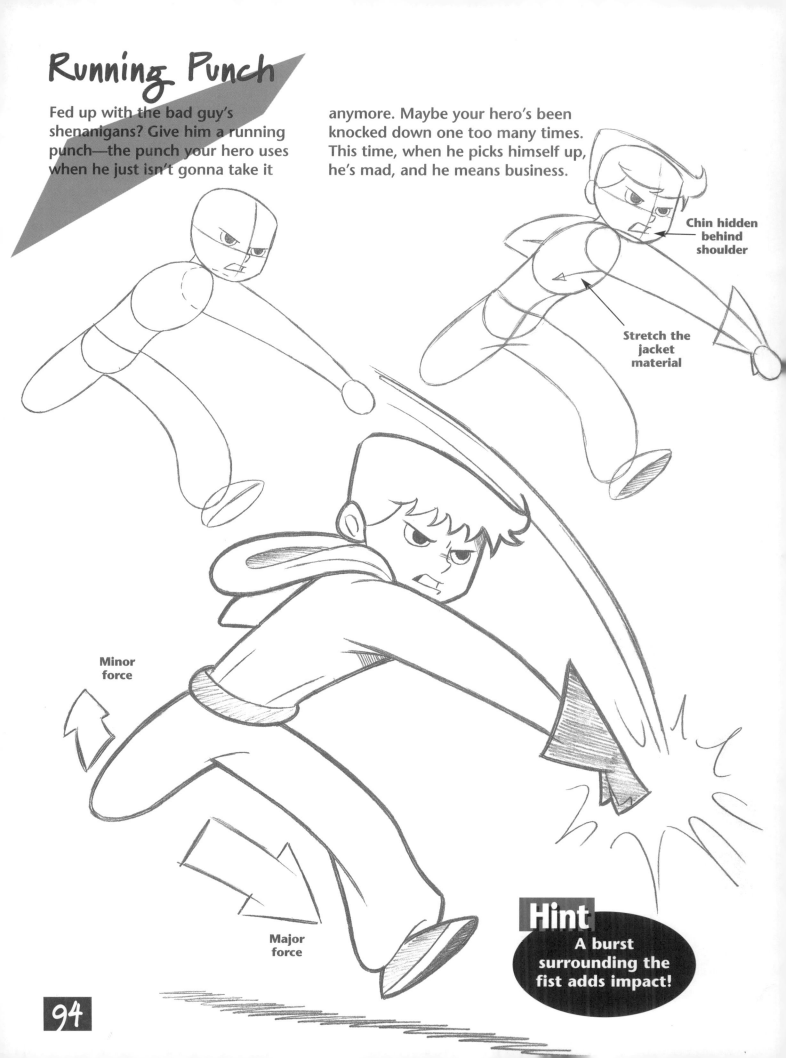

Chin hidden behind shoulder

Stretch the jacket material

Minor force

Major force

Hint
A burst surrounding the fist adds impact!

The Classic Windup

This is the famous windup that precedes the knockout blow. Make it as big and dramatic as the punch itself—in fact, use speed lines to show that the fist is trembling with fury!

Villains can see it coming, but for some reason, they never seem to duck out of the way in time!

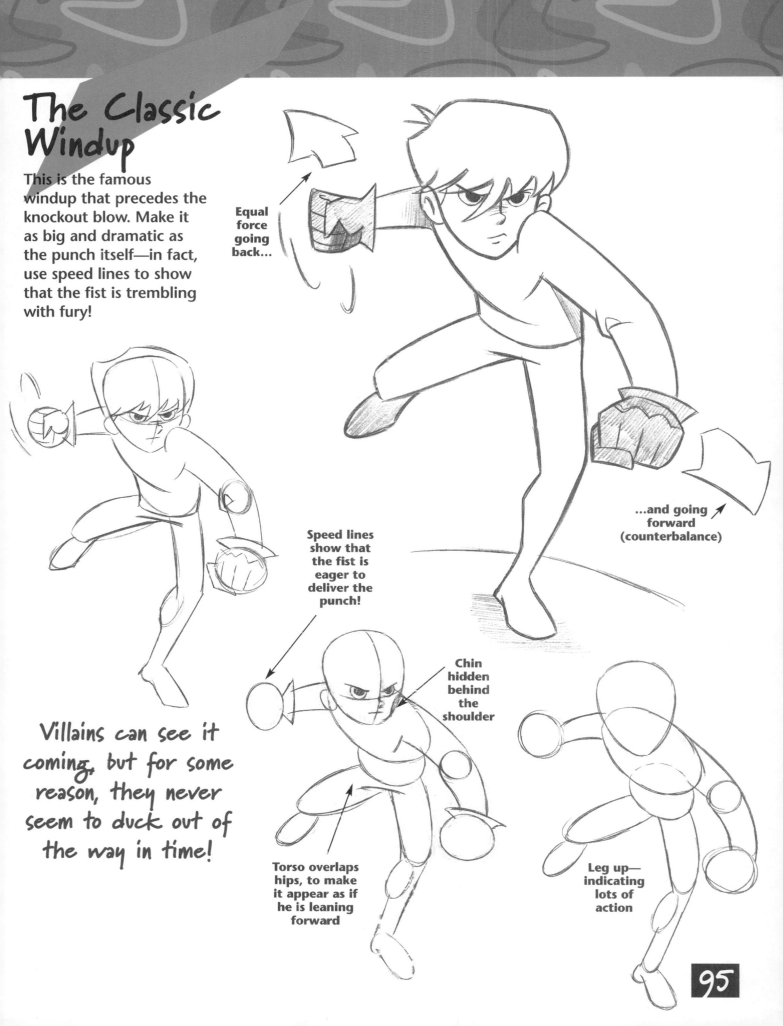

Equal force going back...

...and going forward (counterbalance)

Speed lines show that the fist is eager to deliver the punch!

Chin hidden behind the shoulder

Torso overlaps hips, to make it appear as if he is leaning forward

Leg up— indicating lots of action

MORE FUNNY CHARACTERS

Now we move into the characters section of the book, and boy, have I got some characters for you! We'll take all the principles we've learned so far and use them to create funny characters in all the most popular action-adventure genres: we've got sci-fi soldiers, muscle heroes, even a pirate. And of course, I've included many tips for drawing costumes, helmets and other important space gear.

FACIAL EXPRESSIONS

Here's a drawing trick that comes in handy when designing space characters. To create an expressive face, leave the faceplate off the helmet. And if the character is female, tuck the hair inside the helmet, but allow a good amount of hair to brush across the forehead, in front of the eyes, to give the character a feminine appearance.

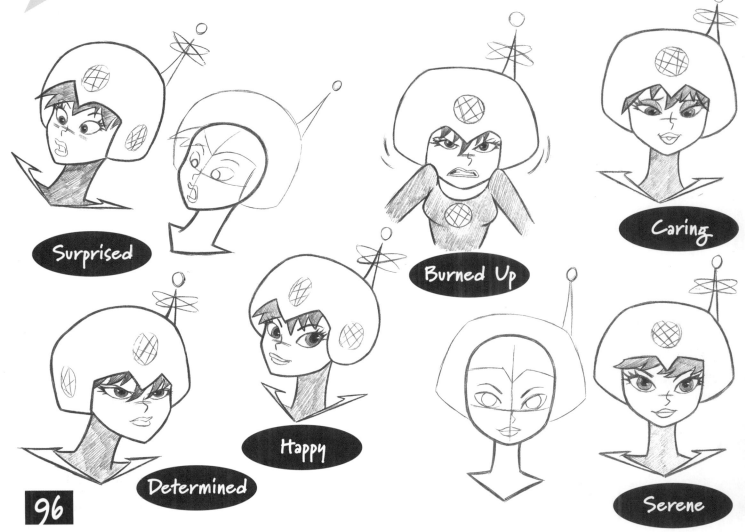

Surprised

Caring

Burned Up

Determined

Happy

Serene

SCI-FI SOLDIERS
The Defender

She may be pretty, but watch out—she's also a great shot. She can take out a dozen enemy fighters at 100 yards.

I'm sure you know just how important costuming is for the sci-fi genre. For female characters, the short, extra-wide skirt with the flared shoulder pads is a classic look. Trendy retro fashions, like these mid-calf boots from the 1960s, always look good.

Drawing the center line down the bridge of the foot makes it easier to find the point at the top of the foot

Never draw realistic guns. One way to avoid the realistic look is to blunt the muzzle, so it looks as if the gun couldn't possible fire bullets, only rays of energy.

The body is three-dimensional —the shading indicates the side view

TWO WAYS OF DRAWING THE ARM

Heavy angle at elbow

Soft angle at elbow

Thigh curves outward

Lower leg curves inward

Foot points to the right

The Yes Man

This space character can be used as a loyal follower, a good commander or an evil warrior. In any role, he's officious and eager to please—to the point of being a real pain.

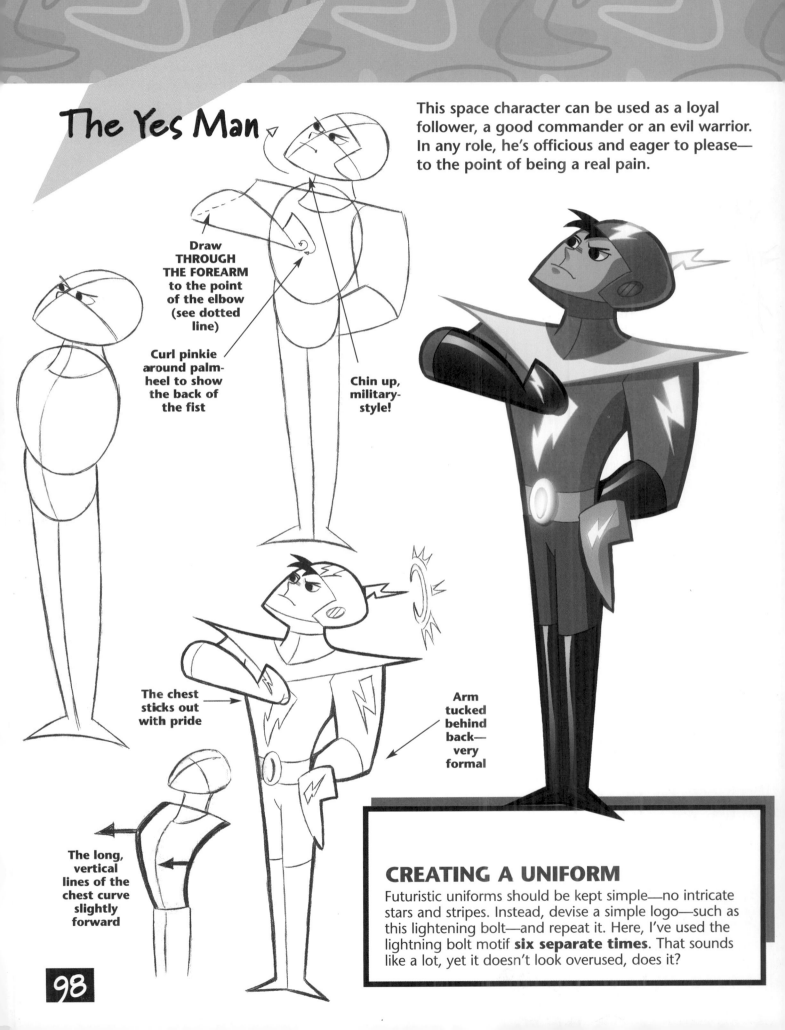

Draw THROUGH THE FOREARM to the point of the elbow (see dotted line)

Curl pinkie around palm-heel to show the back of the fist

Chin up, military-style!

The chest sticks out with pride

Arm tucked behind back—very formal

The long, vertical lines of the chest curve slightly forward

CREATING A UNIFORM

Futuristic uniforms should be kept simple—no intricate stars and stripes. Instead, devise a simple logo—such as this lightening bolt—and repeat it. Here, I've used the lightning bolt motif **six separate times**. That sounds like a lot, yet it doesn't look overused, does it?

Little Toughy

It's the little guy who always has something to prove. Especially if he was born in the reject unit of a spare-parts factory. Looks like this character is missing a few bolts.

I've drawn him from this angle to reinforce his small stature. We are above the little powderkeg, looking down, while he is looking up at us, shaking his fist but intimidating no one.

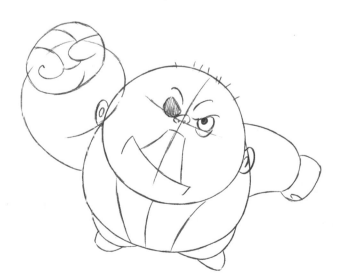

DRAWING AN EXTREME DOWN ANGLE

When drawing an angle at this *extreme view*—also called a "bird's-eye view," the way to do it is to overlap layer upon layer—and then it becomes easy. Take a look:

The head (A) overlaps the torso (B), which overlaps the legs (C), which overlap the feet (D).

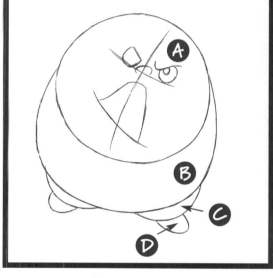

SPACE ADVENTURERS

Humorous futuristic cartoons are always popular with TV audiences, because the characters are quirky, inventive and fanciful. And for my money, the young characters—kids in particular—are the funniest.

For a young character, place the eye line low on the head

Space Boy

Make him short and pudgy, which is a funny shape for an intergalactic fighter. Notice that his head is practically the same height as his body—and even wider!

Pear-shaped body

Inner leg line drawn as a single, arching line

Make sure there's ample room between face and helmet, so it looks comfortable, not cramped

Carve out the face for a three-quarter view

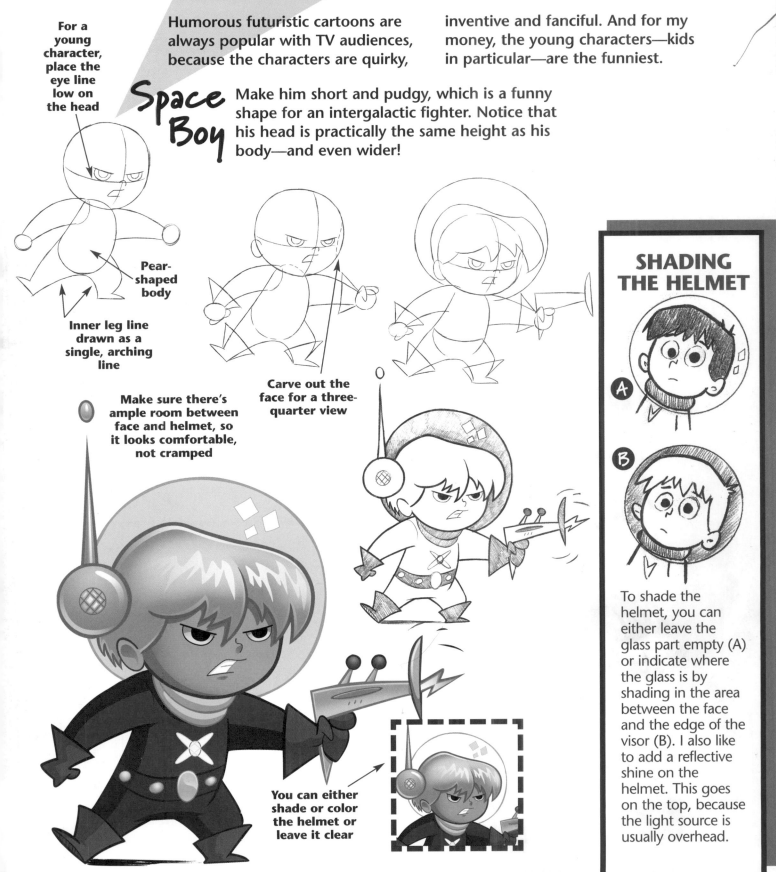

You can either shade or color the helmet or leave it clear

SHADING THE HELMET

A

B

To shade the helmet, you can either leave the glass part empty (A) or indicate where the glass is by shading in the area between the face and the edge of the visor (B). I also like to add a reflective shine on the helmet. This goes on the top, because the light source is usually overhead.

Timid Space Explorer

Okay, so he's set the flag down on another planet and claimed it for the earth, like he was supposed to. So how come the spaceship just took off without him?

The timid type—also known as the overwhelmed character—is funniest if he looks like he's wearing a hand-me-down suit that's two sizes too big. Look at those gloves—they look like potholders! Note the giant, perfectly round pupils. They give him the famous puppy-dog eyes that immediately gain our sympathy.

Draw ears very low and flappy to emphasize the character's youth

Neck swimming inside bigger body shape

Body is an easy single shape

Head is a simple oval without modification

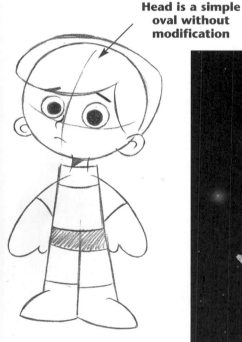

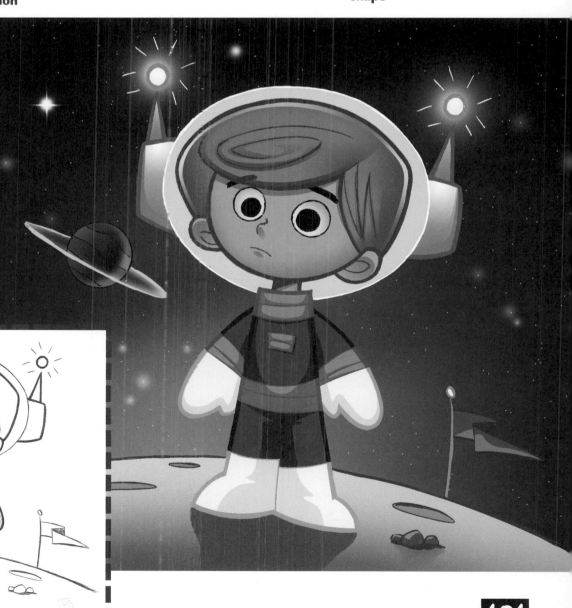

Making Friends with a "Space-Boing"

Here's your chance to get extra-imaginative by creating an entirely new creature. But keep it simple! Simple is funnier than complicated. Notice anything funny here?

What's the girl doing with a helmet that doesn't surround her head? What if the planet doesn't have oxygen!? In cartoons, we don't worry about technicalities like breathing.

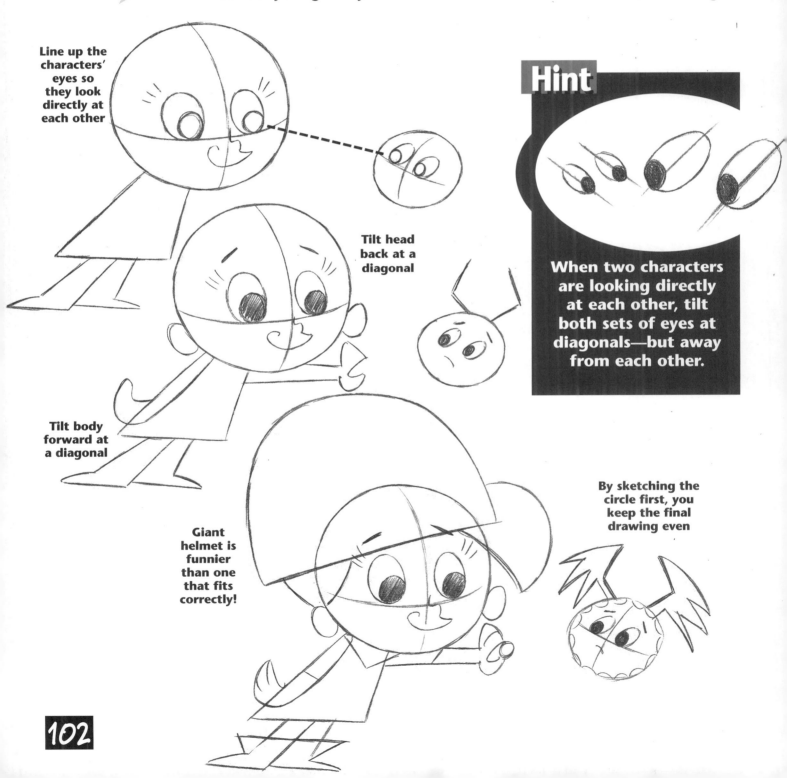

Line up the characters' eyes so they look directly at each other

Hint

When two characters are looking directly at each other, tilt both sets of eyes at diagonals—but away from each other.

Tilt head back at a diagonal

Tilt body forward at a diagonal

Giant helmet is funnier than one that fits correctly!

By sketching the circle first, you keep the final drawing even

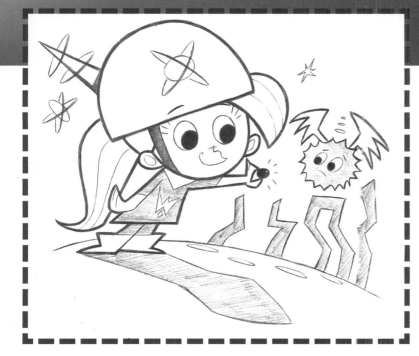

Everyone should have a pet, even if it lives north of Neptune.

MUSCLE-BOUND HERO

These muscle-bound do-gooders mean well, but they're bumbling lunkheads who make crime really pay for bad guys. Draw these fun characters as if they were blown up like balloons and have trouble even bending their limbs due to all that muscle. And remember the law of inverse muscular development: the bigger the biceps, the smaller the brain!

Note the downward sloping curve of all the major horizontal lines

The blue line shows the major muscle groups of the upper torso: the chest "shields" and abdominal walls.

Front View

Our cartoon muscle hero has huge arms and small legs. When he stands before us, he should look immense. To exaggerate this effect, make it look as though you are looking up at him. You accomplish this by drawing the horizontal lines curving slightly downward (see arrows). That gives the figure its awesome, towering look.

Side View

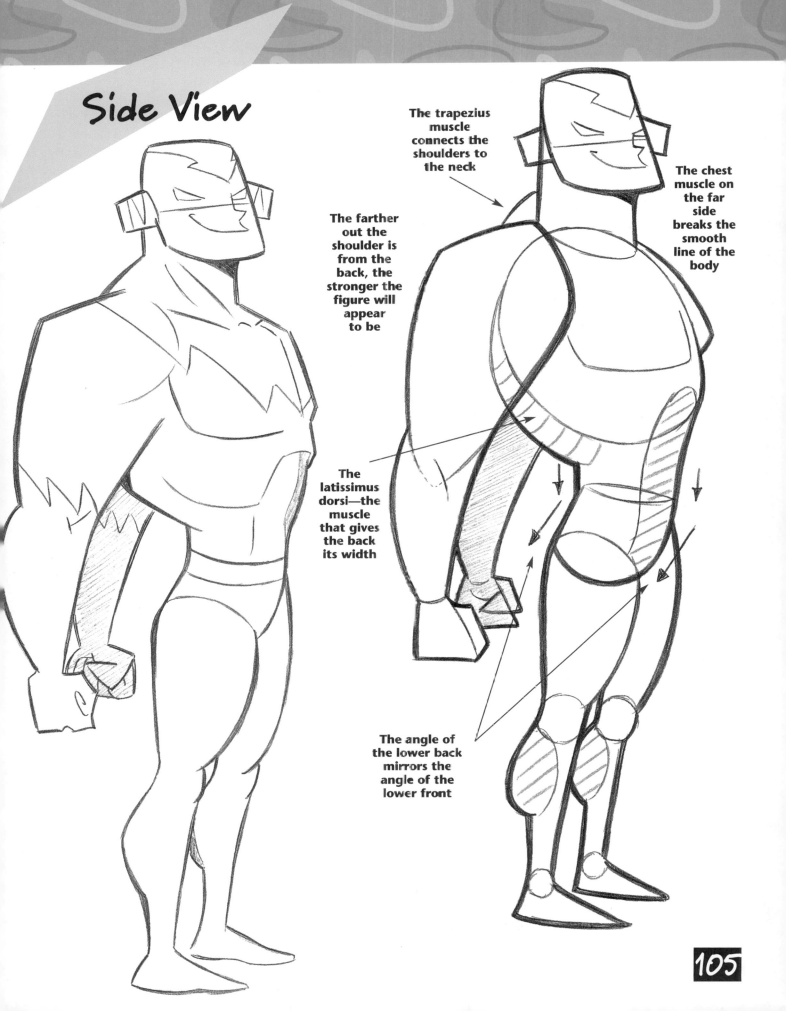

The trapezius muscle connects the shoulders to the neck

The chest muscle on the far side breaks the smooth line of the body

The farther out the shoulder is from the back, the stronger the figure will appear to be

The latissimus dorsi—the muscle that gives the back its width

The angle of the lower back mirrors the angle of the lower front

Back View

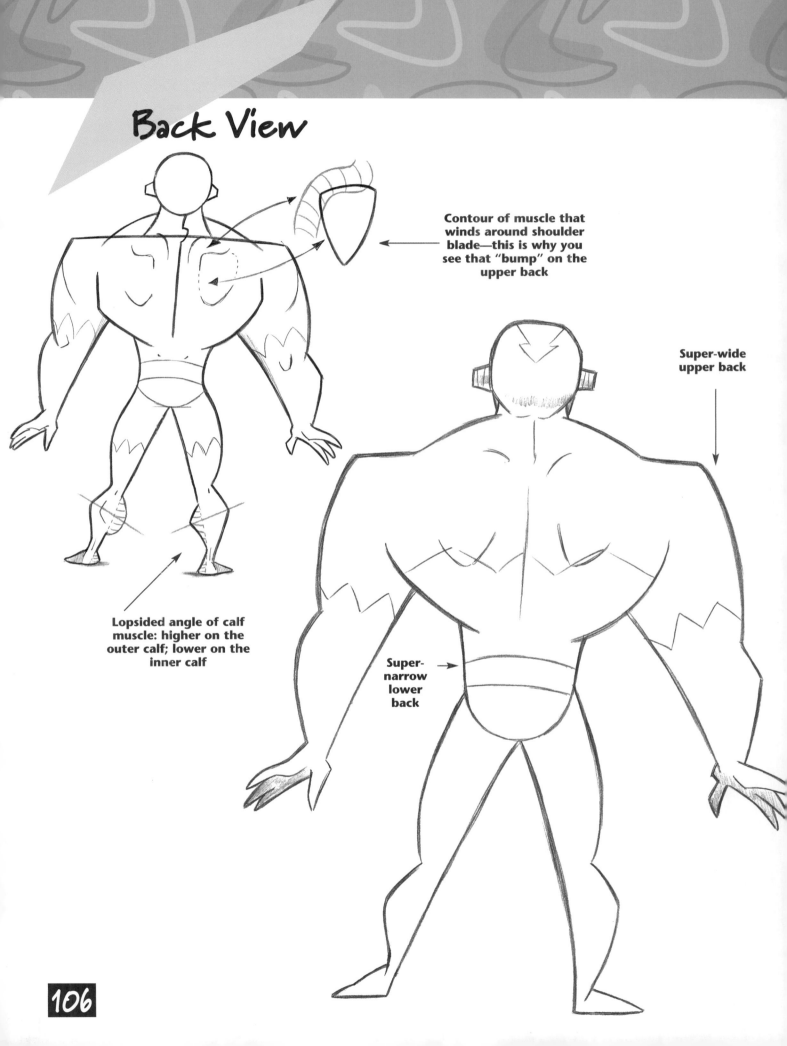

Contour of muscle that winds around shoulder blade—this is why you see that "bump" on the upper back

Super-wide upper back

Lopsided angle of calf muscle: higher on the outer calf; lower on the inner calf

Super-narrow lower back

Gesture Sketches

Gesture sketches are an important part of honing your drawing skills. They're a way of getting the essence of a pose without drawing the details. Gesture sketching is ideal for transferring the excitement of an idea down on paper. Draw them fast and loose. Once you have your sketch, use it as the basis for your finished drawing.

Hint

Note how I've used the two most important action lines in these sketches: the vertical center line and the horizontal chest line. Be sure to really *bend and stretch* these action lines to give the gestures a sense of purpose and feeling!

Super-Feet!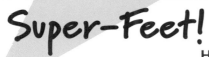

How can someone with such overgrown muscles have such skinny little feet? Beats me! But it's been a comic book convention since way back. So draw them long, narrow and floppy, coming to a soft point at the tips.

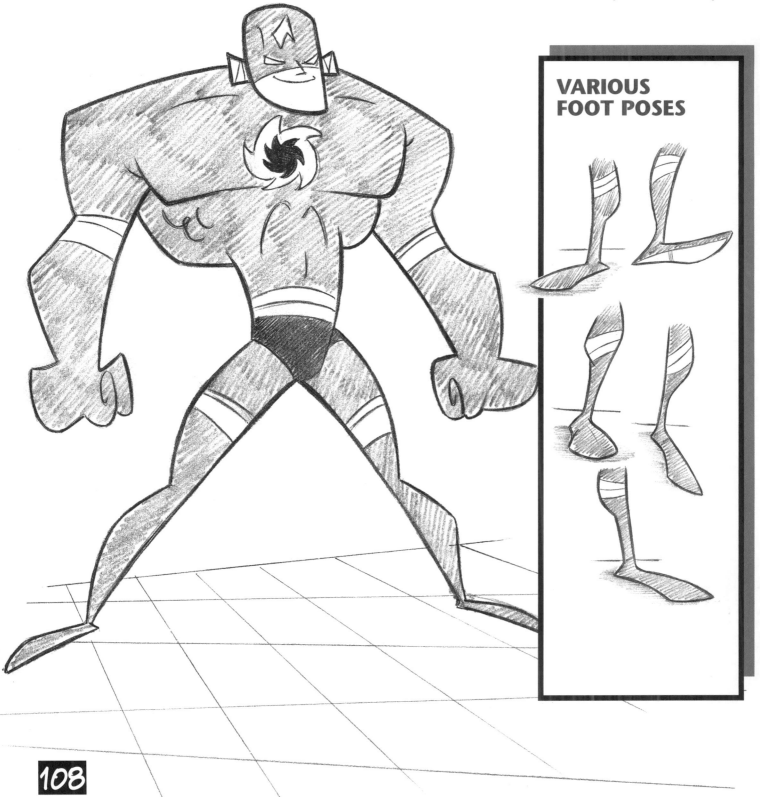

VARIOUS FOOT POSES

Action Poses

The action line doesn't have to travel through any particular place on the body—not through a leg, an arm or even the spine or the head. Draw it wherever you find the major thrust of the pose.

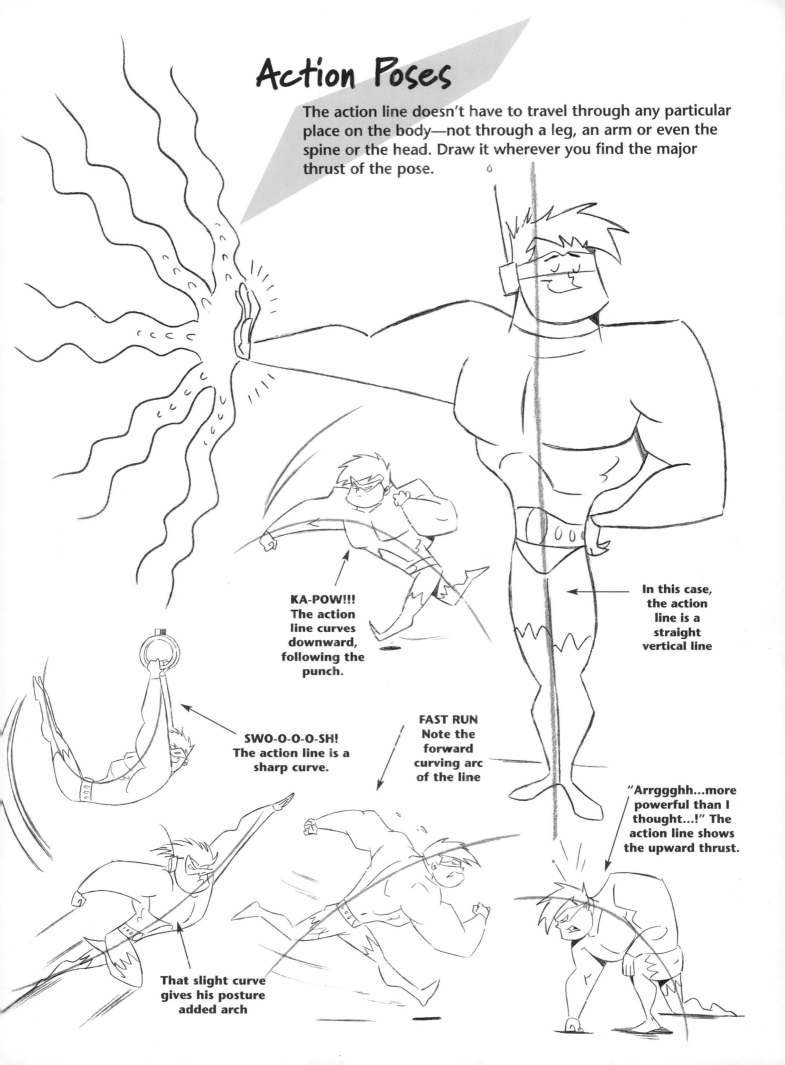

KA-POW!!! The action line curves downward, following the punch.

SWO-O-O-O-SH! The action line is a sharp curve.

FAST RUN Note the forward curving arc of the line

In this case, the action line is a straight vertical line

"Arrggghh...more powerful than I thought...!" The action line shows the upward thrust.

That slight curve gives his posture added arch

NARCISSISTIC HERO

Love those muscles! With this much self-admiration, he could run for governor of California. This character is totally humorous and barely ever found in truly dangerous situations. In fact, you could even cast him as an introvert who's shy when he's not posing.

This type of goofy character is always drawn in a very cartoony style. Have fun with him, and don't worry about real anatomy!

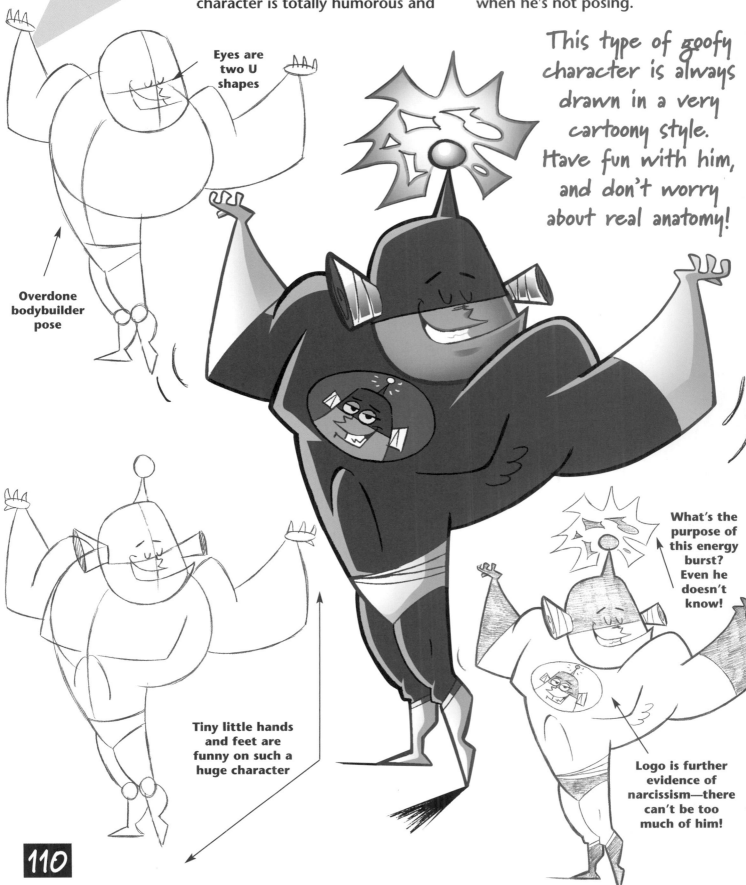

Eyes are two U shapes

Overdone bodybuilder pose

Tiny little hands and feet are funny on such a huge character

What's the purpose of this energy burst? Even he doesn't know!

Logo is further evidence of narcissism—there can't be too much of him!

FLASHY HERO

This guy gets a lot of his style from his extremely tapered build. In addition, the opposing straight and curved lines of his arms and legs are emphasized to a great degree. Third, his pose is one of extreme confidence— and not just because of the clenched fist or the foot position, but also because of the chest-out stance. And last, the flared shoulders are a sharp addition to the costume.

The position of the arms dictates whether the lines will be straight or bumpy

Note the extensive line work used to create the rhythm and flow of the legs

"MASKED" HERO

I always find this style of costume funny. I mean, what's the purpose of all that material? It covers almost all of his head, yet there's no disguise!

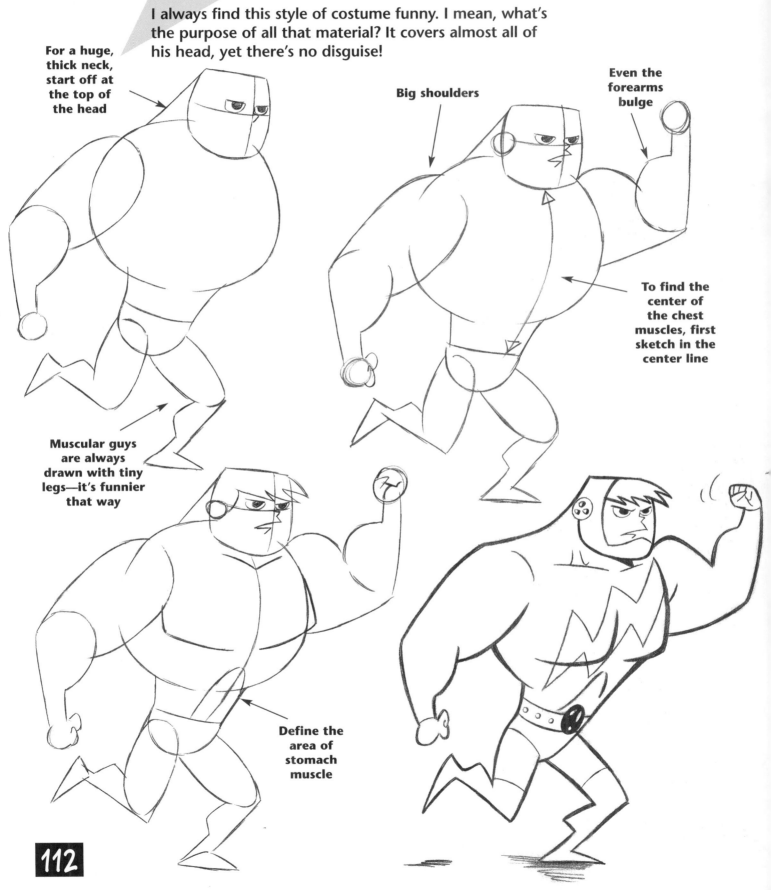

For a huge, thick neck, start off at the top of the head

Big shoulders

Even the forearms bulge

To find the center of the chest muscles, first sketch in the center line

Muscular guys are always drawn with tiny legs—it's funnier that way

Define the area of stomach muscle

112

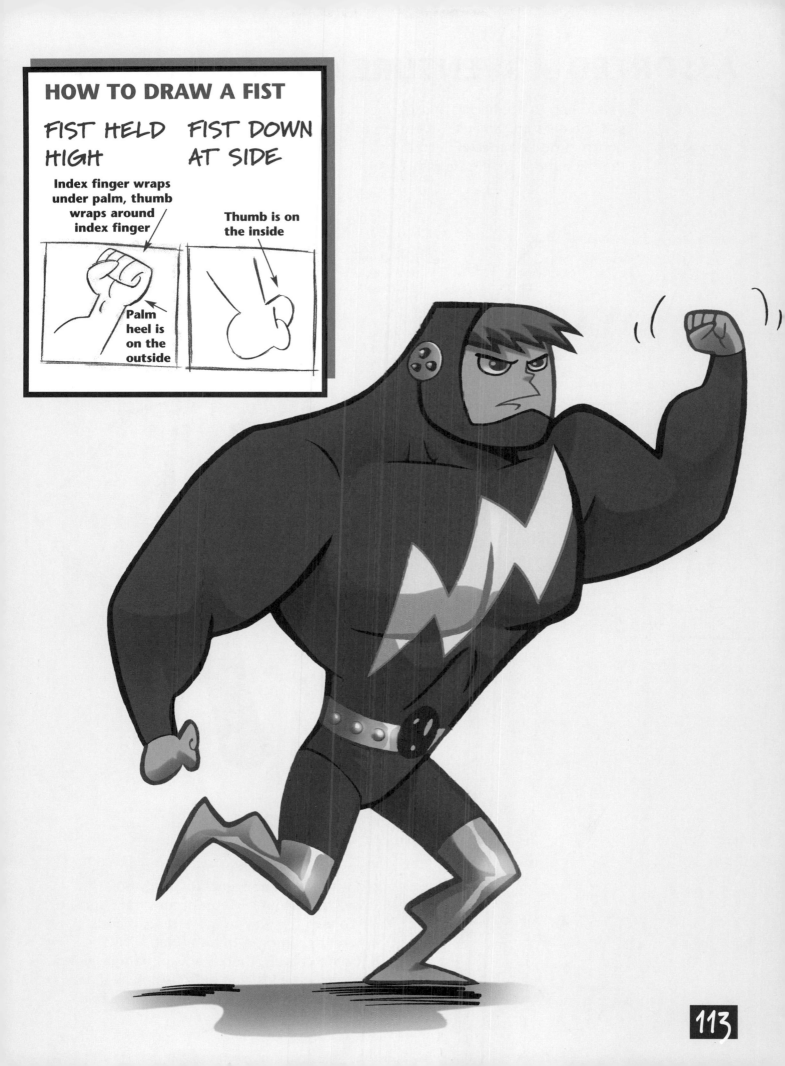

HOW TO DRAW A FIST

FIST HELD HIGH

FIST DOWN AT SIDE

Index finger wraps under palm, thumb wraps around index finger

Palm heel is on the outside

Thumb is on the inside

ASSORTED ADVENTURE CHARACTERS

In addition to the heroes, muscle men, evil scientists and spy gals, there are a bunch of other appealing characters that fill out the adventure cast. Each type doesn't necessarily warrant his or her own individual chapter, but they're a lot of fun to draw, so we'll group them together here.

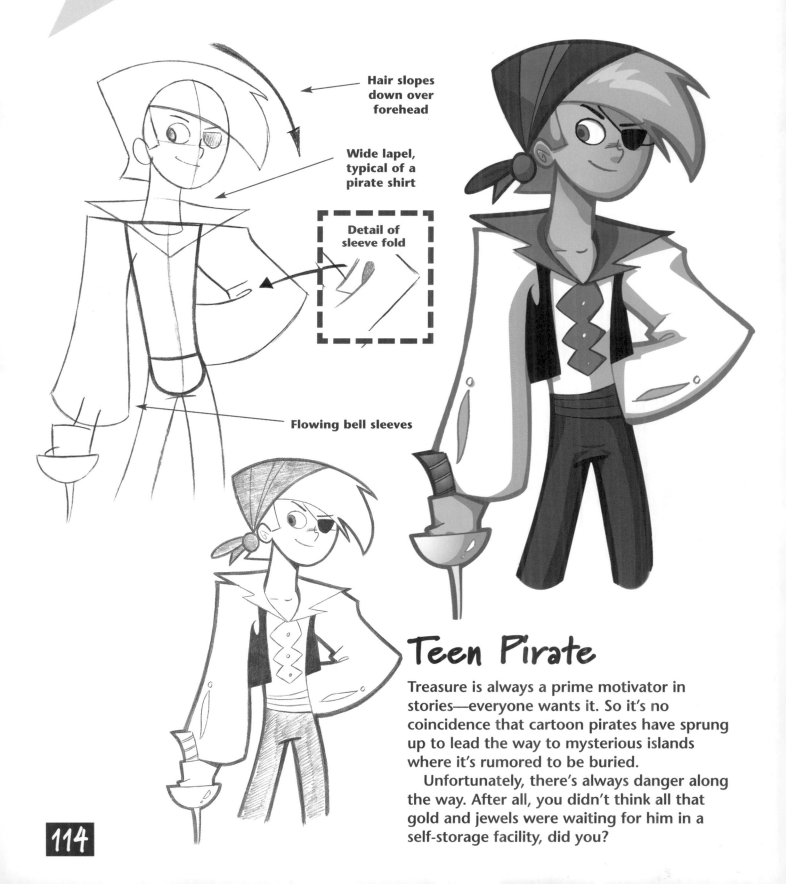

Hair slopes down over forehead

Wide lapel, typical of a pirate shirt

Detail of sleeve fold

Flowing bell sleeves

Teen Pirate

Treasure is always a prime motivator in stories—everyone wants it. So it's no coincidence that cartoon pirates have sprung up to lead the way to mysterious islands where it's rumored to be buried.

Unfortunately, there's always danger along the way. After all, you didn't think all that gold and jewels were waiting for him in a self-storage facility, did you?

Island Princess

A hurricane whips your pirate's little craft hundreds of miles off course. Sharks tear the hull to pieces, and the tide sweeps him onto some unknown island where his host is...(drumroll, please) Princess Hanna Lanna. Give her an exotic outfit complete with a jeweled headpiece and gold earrings and necklace.

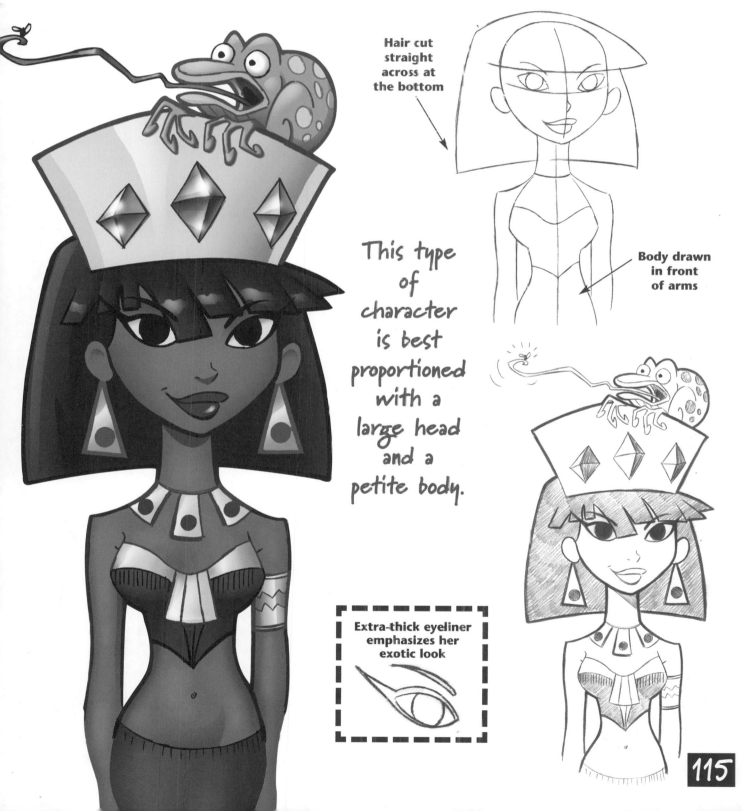

Hair cut straight across at the bottom

Body drawn in front of arms

This type of character is best proportioned with a large head and a petite body.

Extra-thick eyeliner emphasizes her exotic look

Cool Gal

Can't you see her cruising down Rodeo Drive in a ragtop, ponytails blowing in the breeze? Here's a great example of how a stylish cartoon isn't necessarily difficult to draw. This one is a snap: the entire head is based on a simple egg shape. Add the center line and an eye line, and the rest is just filling in the features.

Leave lots of room for forehead

The eyes are spaced wide apart

Nose and mouth are placed low on the face

Darken eyelids

High School Reject

These are the tough years. You get rejected by girls, rejected by the varsity team, even rejected by the chess team because you're not cool enough. But because you've never lost a game of rock-paper-scissors, you've been discovered by the Secret Service, which is looking for someone who can bluff the world's most wanted super-villain. Now you're cool!

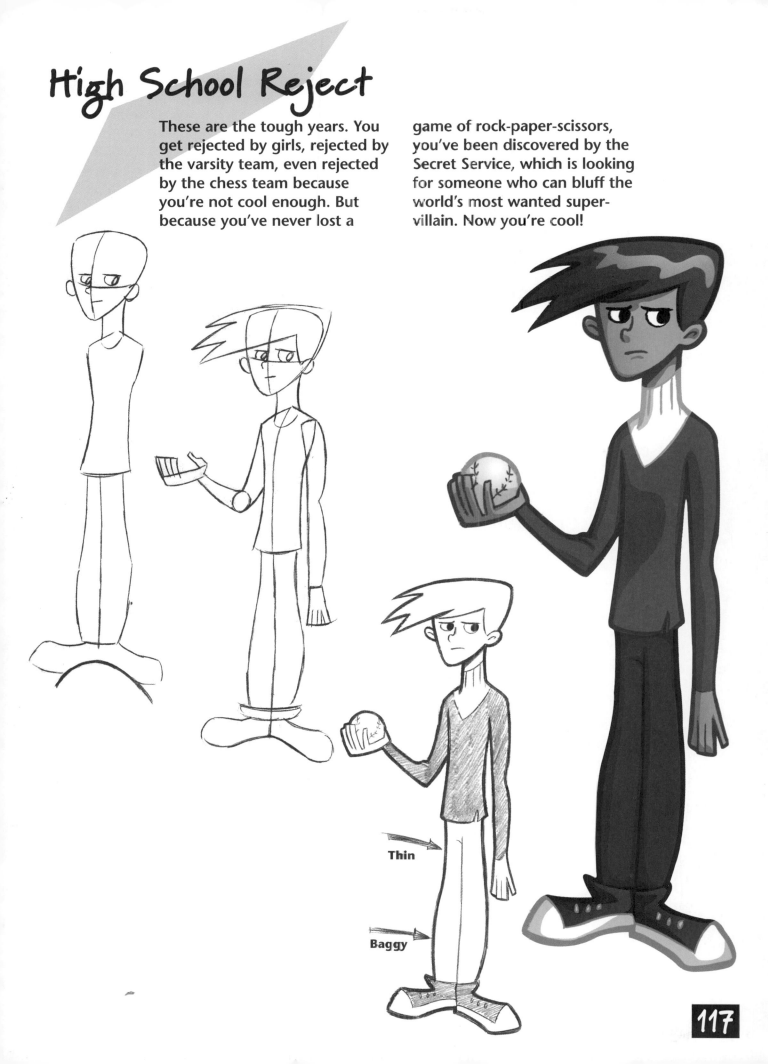

Thin

Baggy

Secret Weapons Spy

Any prop can turn into a spy device or weapon. Gadgets are the most fun when camouflaged as everyday objects that suddenly transform into technical contraptions. Keep some of their original form after the transformation to maintain the humor.

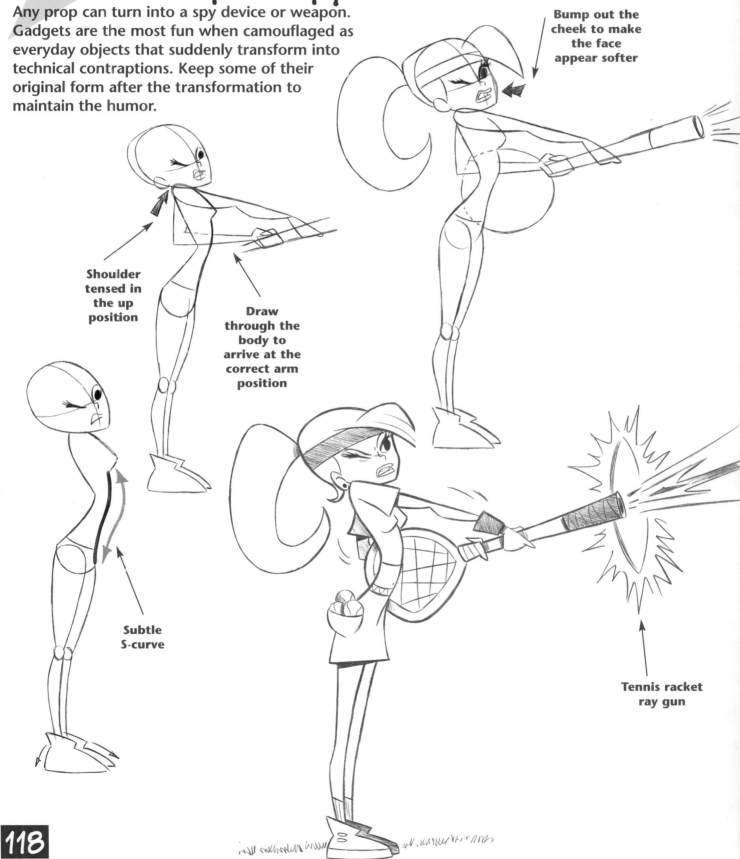

Bump out the cheek to make the face appear softer

Shoulder tensed in the up position

Draw through the body to arrive at the correct arm position

Subtle S-curve

Tennis racket ray gun

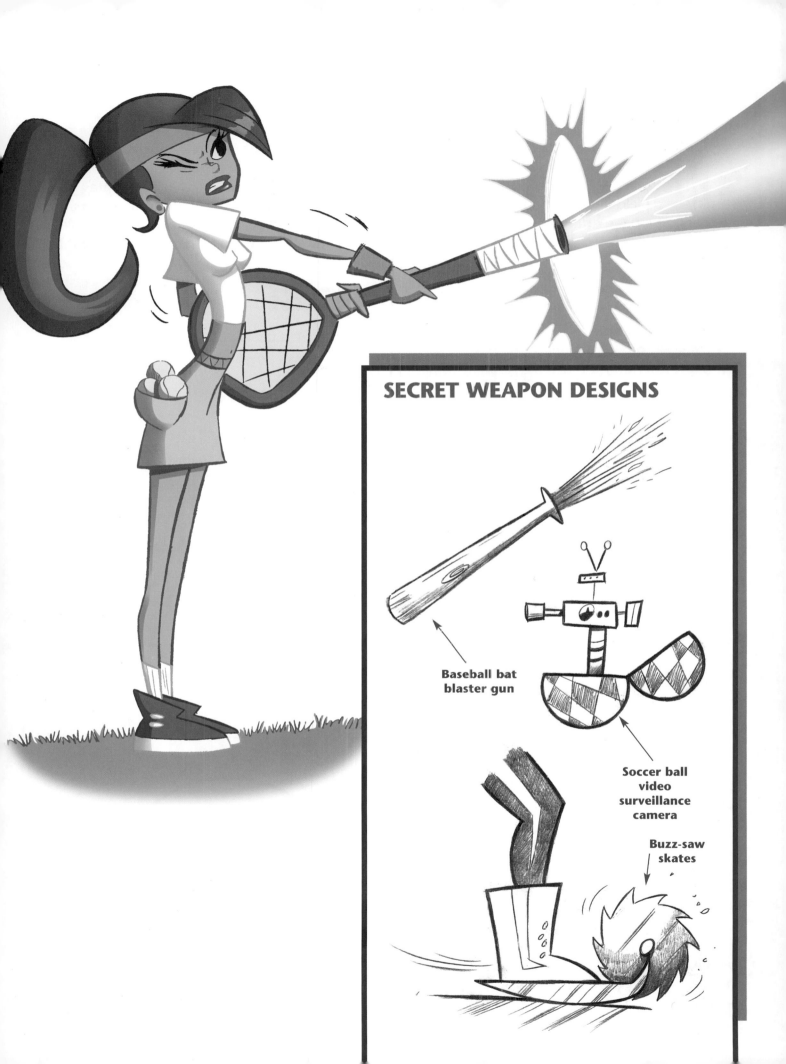

SECRET WEAPON DESIGNS

Baseball bat
blaster gun

Soccer ball
video
surveillance
camera

Buzz-saw
skates

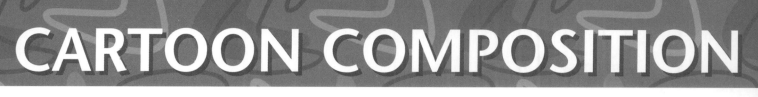

CARTOON COMPOSITION

Now let's take some of these characters you've been learning to draw—and some original ones you may have been developing—and learn how to place them on a page or in panels for maximum impact. You'll learn that you don't always need to draw the entire figure—sometimes closeups or medium shots are more powerful than full shots. Further, you'll see that sometimes, certain types of closeups work better than others.

Here are some basic composition principles that will show off your drawings in the best light.

FRAMING YOUR CHARACTER

When a character is facing in one direction or another, don't place him or her in the middle of the frame. Instead, leave more space in the direction that he is facing. Doesn't it look more natural like this?

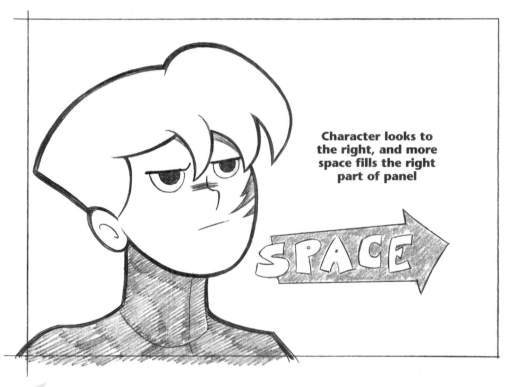

Character looks to the right, and more space fills the right part of panel

SPACE

Composing a Closeup

How close can you go in for a closeup? One popular method is to cut off the mouth in order to give the most emphasis to the eyes. But it's still important to leave a comfortable amount of room around the head. In other words, leave ample room between the borders of the panel and the outline of the head.

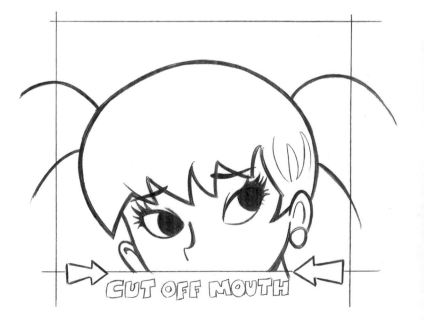

CUT OFF MOUTH

Extreme Closeup

Can't get much closer than this, or more intense. In a shot like this, you can really focus on the character's emotions. And boy, is he ticked off. In this kind of shot, you come in so close that you focus on only one eye. But even so, always leave some room around the head, between the hair and the borders of the panel.

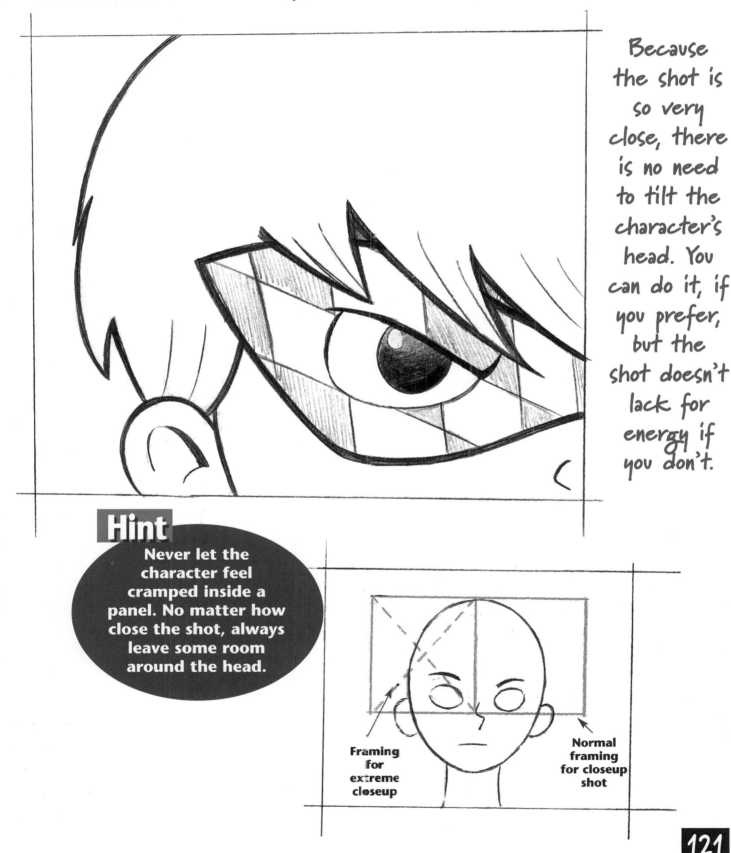

Because the shot is so very close, there is no need to tilt the character's head. You can do it, if you prefer, but the shot doesn't lack for energy if you don't.

Hint

Never let the character feel cramped inside a panel. No matter how close the shot, always leave some room around the head.

Framing for extreme closeup

Normal framing for closeup shot

121

HORIZON LINES

Placing the Horizon Line

The word "horizontal" comes from "horizon." A horizon line that goes straight across a scene is a calming, soothing sight, because that's what we expect to see. Therefore, for action scenes, where you want the effect to be anything but calm, draw the horizon line at a diagonal instead of horizontally.

The horizon line isn't used only outdoors, where the sky meets the ground. It's also used in interior scenes where the wall meets the floor. A character drawn in a full-length shot needs a horizon line behind him. Otherwise, he'll appear to be floating.

Intense horizon line

Calm horizon line

Drawing Without a Horizon Line

A character drawn in a medium shot, as shown here, doesn't require a horizon line. In fact, it's best avoided, as it tends to flatten out the scene.

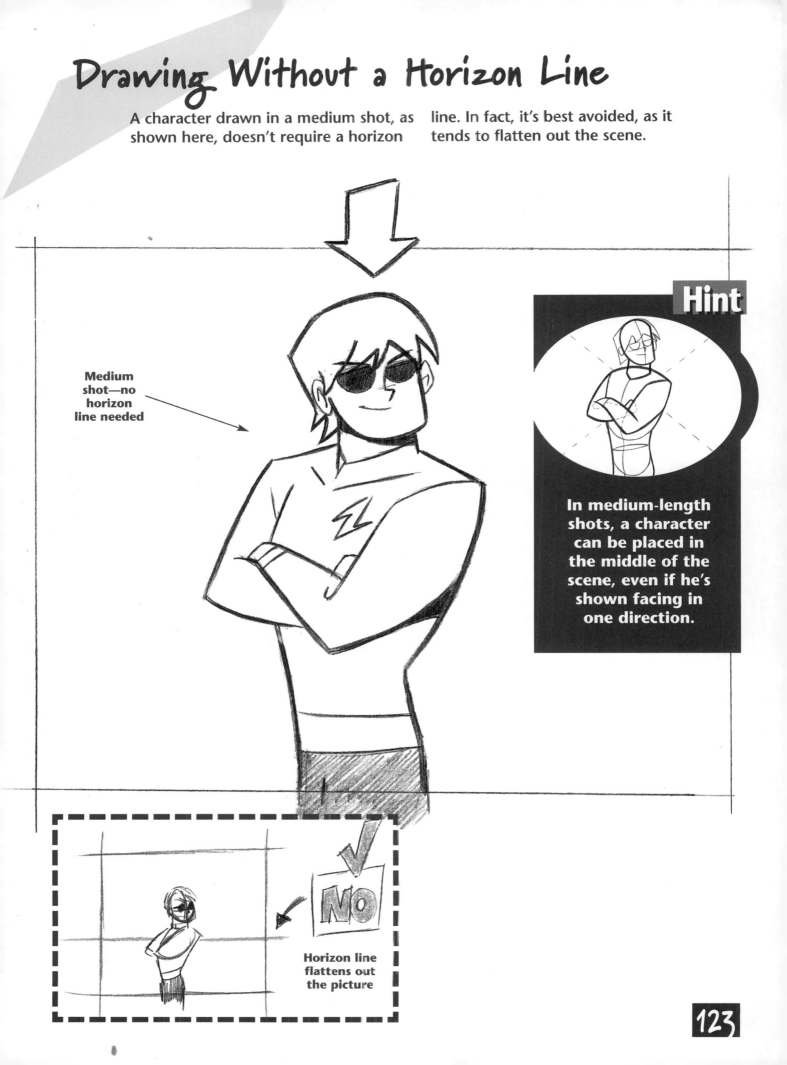

Medium shot—no horizon line needed

Hint

In medium-length shots, a character can be placed in the middle of the scene, even if he's shown facing in one direction.

NO

Horizon line flattens out the picture

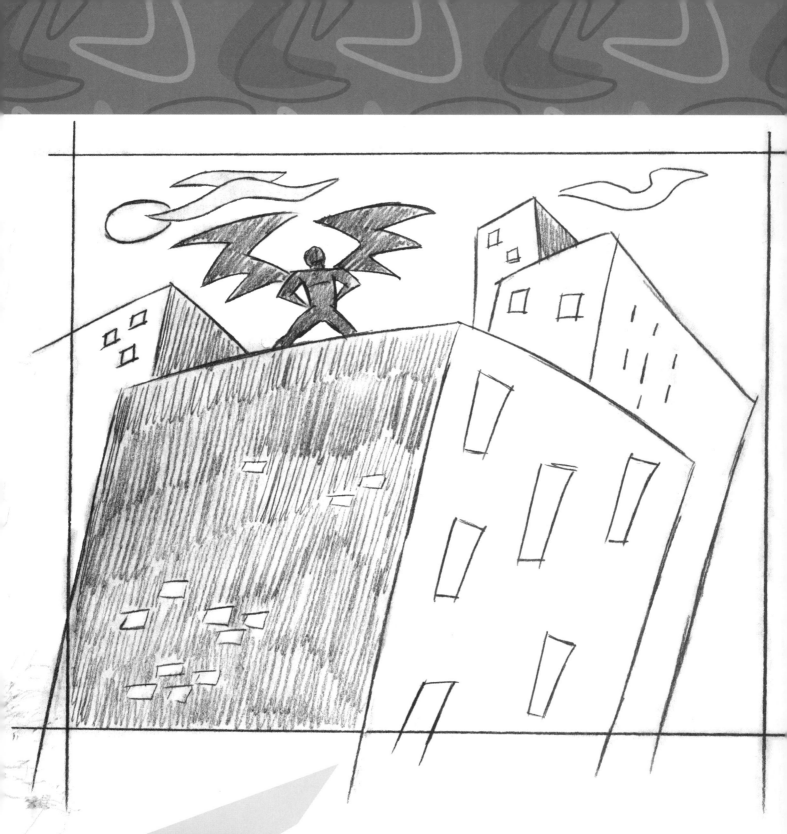

LONG SHOTS

Characters shown in long shots are portrayed very dramatically, by nature. They are often shown in silhouette and overlapped by large, imposing foregrounds. In addition, they typically appear in the top or bottom third of the panel. I recommend that you **avoid** placing a character in the middle of the panel. Frankly, that's kind of boring.

TANGENTS

A tangent is the spot where the edge of a character touches the edge of something else in a scene, unintentionally. Animators are taught to avoid this as if it were the worst thing in the world. It's not. No kid ever walked out of an animated movie and said, "I loved it! But those tangents really blew it for me."

However, in comic book panels it's deadly to create a tangent by allowing a character to touch the borders of the panel. You see, the **border** isn't supposed to **really exist**. It's sort of a make-believe wall. But when a character touches it, it suddenly becomes real, and then it looks weird to the reader, making it difficult for him to suspend his disbelief and get back into the story. And it also makes the character look CRAMPED in the panel, something that's always a no-no!

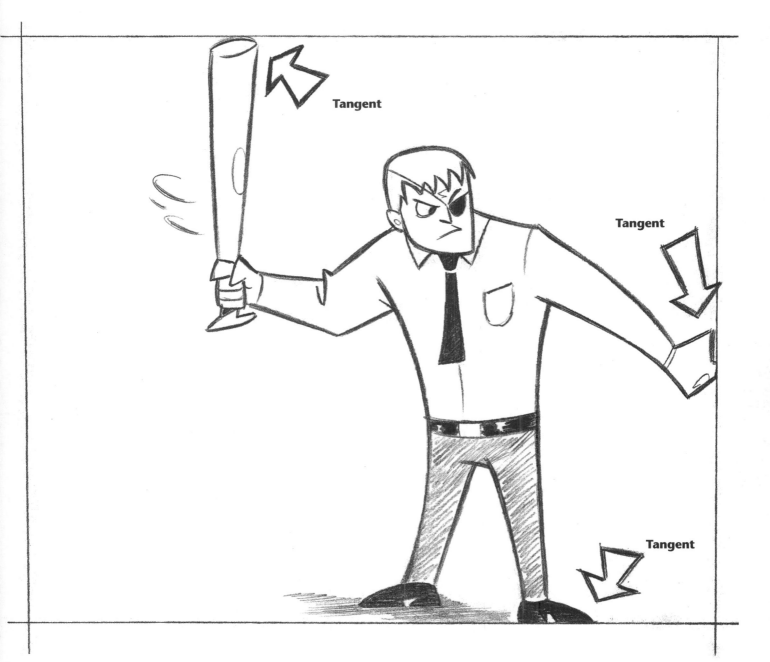

Tangent

Tangent

Tangent

LIGHTING

Let's take a look at the two most common lighting effects: light from above (sky and ceiling lights) and light from below (scary lighting effects).

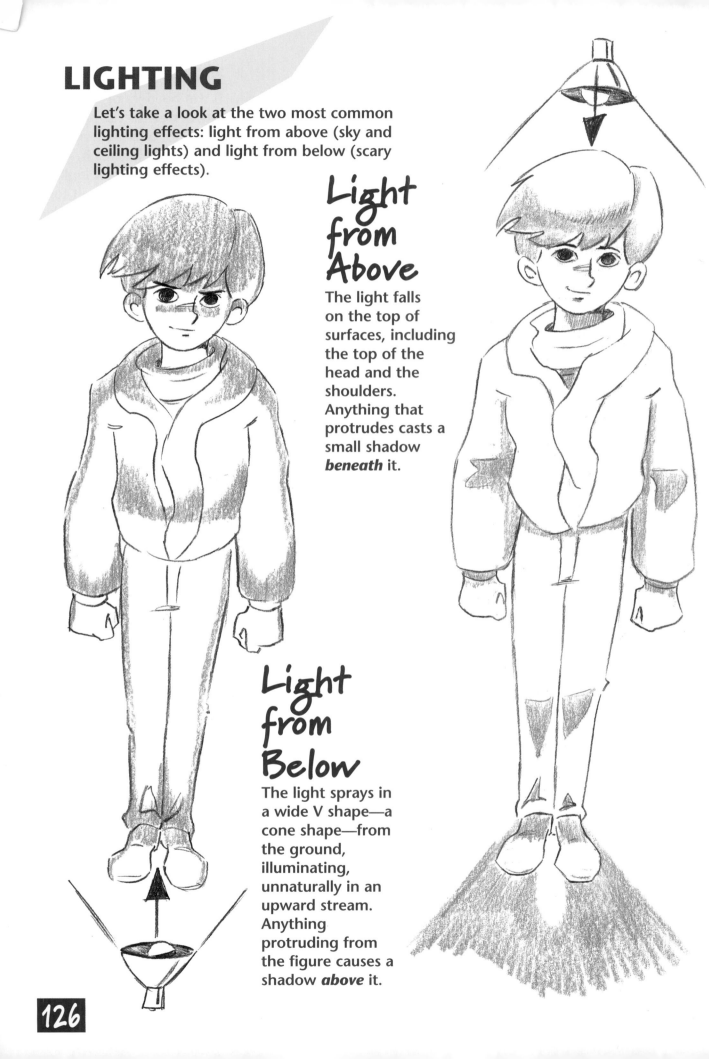

Light from Above

The light falls on the top of surfaces, including the top of the head and the shoulders. Anything that protrudes casts a small shadow **beneath** it.

Light from Below

The light sprays in a wide V shape—a cone shape—from the ground, illuminating, unnaturally in an upward stream. Anything protruding from the figure causes a shadow **above** it.

Dramatic Lighting Effects

To make lighting dramatic, you have to have shadows! In everyday life, light is generally omnidirectional, meaning that it is all around us, casting its glow evenly, which eliminates shadows. To create dramatic lighting, give the light a specific direction so that it will cast a shadow.

The most popular and effective method is to shine the light from the side. This will cause shadows to fall heavily on the character.

Light sources left and right hit character simultaneously

Shining light from the left and right sides simultaneously makes the shadows fall directly in the center of the figure and creates an intense look.

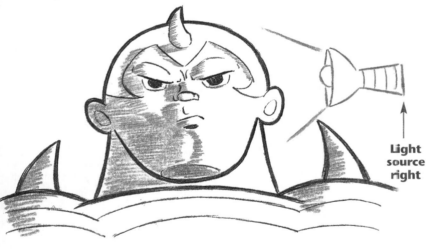

Light source right

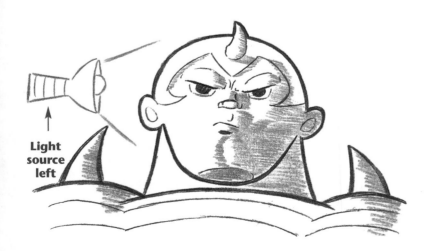

Light source left

YOU CAN DRAW LIKE A PRO!

I've enjoyed sharing these techniques with you. Adventure-style cartoon characters are some of the most fun to draw. And now that you've got the same tools as the pros, you can come up with your own original adventure-style characters.

Thanks for visiting, and until next time, keep drawing!

Chris Hart

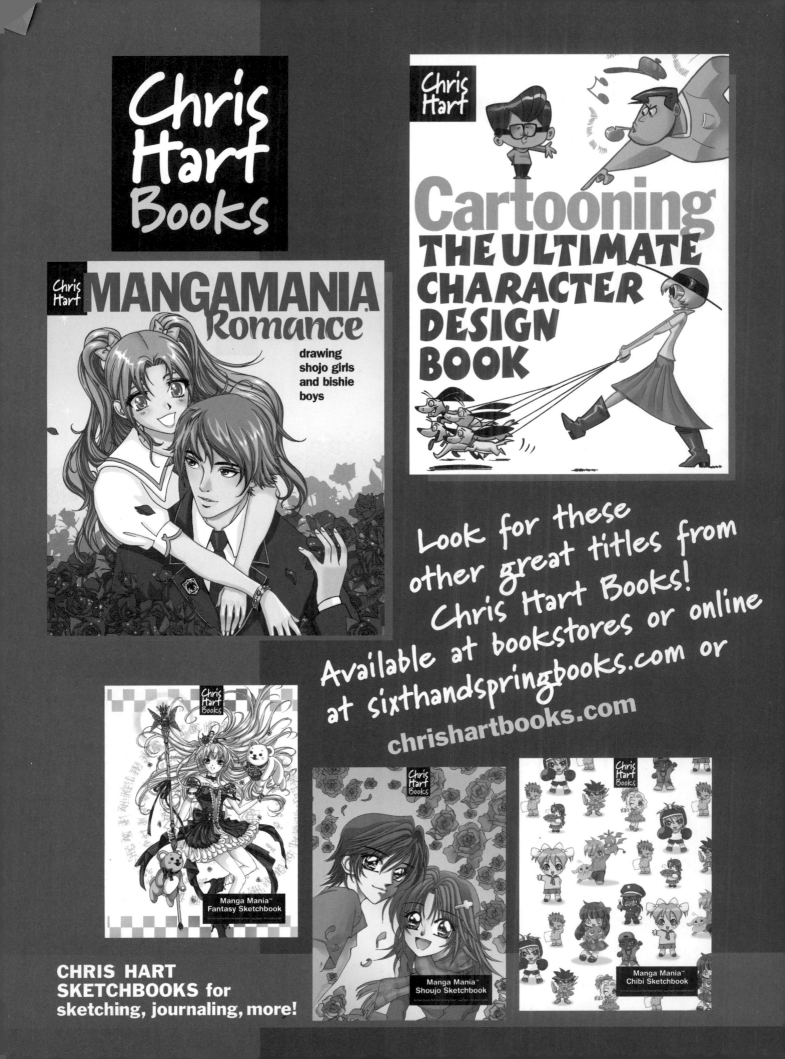